Review for other
chpt

School Council Inquiry

23 . 6 . 78

Curriculum Development in Physical Education

This book is one of a series on physical education edited by

John E. Kane, M.Ed., Ph.D.

Principal, Loughborough College of Education, and
Professor, Loughborough University of Technology.
Formerly Director of Physical Education, University of
Leeds.

Other titles in this series include

Exercise Physiology by Vaughan Thomas
The Mechanics of Human Movement by B. J. Hopper

Curriculum Development in Physical Education

Edited by John E. Kane, M.Ed., Ph.D.

Crosby Lockwood Staples   London

Granada Publishing Limited
First published in Great Britain 1976 by
Crosby Lockwood Staples
Frogmore St Albans Herts
and 3 Upper James Street London W1R 4BP

ISBN 0 258 96985 7

Filmset in Photon Times 12 pt by
Richard Clay (The Chaucer Press), Ltd, Bungay, Suffolk
and printed in Great Britain by
Fletcher & Son Ltd, Norwich

Contributors

Leonard Almond, M.A.
Curriculum Research
Fellow, Loughborough
College of Education.

Peter C. McIntosh, M.A
Professor and Director,
School of Physical
Education, University of
Otago.

Alan Gibbon, M.A.
Inspector of Physical
Education, Inner London
Education Authority.

Peter Renshaw, M.A.
Lecturer in Education,
Institute of Education,
University of Leeds.

John E. Kane, M.Ed., Ph.D.
Principal, Loughborough
College of Education, and
Professor, Loughborough
University of Technology.

Neville J. Whitehead,
M.Ed., Ph.D.
Principal Lecturer in
Physical Education, City of
Leeds and Carnegie College
of Education.

Contents

Introduction

The last ten years or so have seen a veritable curriculum
revolution in Britain associated, no doubt, with the developing impact of the Schools Council set up in 1964 for the
purpose of reviewing and reforming the curriculum. The
momentum and pace of the curriculum reform movement
since then have been so impressive that even its most
enthusiastic advocates have been taken by surprise. As with
all such revolutions in education, there is an emphatic need
to scrutinise carefully the claims being made for the new
approaches and systems by the enthusiastic innovators—
who often unwittingly carry with them, in bandwagon fashion, their committed supporters and imitators. Progress towards a worthwhile curriculum renewal requires knowledge
and understanding more than enthusiasm; rational and
coherent planning more than commitment. If, as it seems,
the effects of the curriculum reform movement have come
relatively late to physical education, a serious consideration
of curriculum renewal in this area should no longer be
delayed. However, as a late entrant to the field of curriculum
reform, physical education has one special advantage: it is
possible to assess critically the application to this 'subject' of
numerous earlier curriculum experiments. This book has
been planned therefore to review current trends in curriculum reform and to consider their application to physical
education.

Chapter 1 makes it clear that this area of the curriculum
has changed a great deal since 1870: as McIntosh puts it,

'Physical education has developed from simple military drill to a variegated and bewildering pattern of activities'. The nature and educational meaning of this 'bewildering pattern' is currently being subjected to a fundamental reappraisal— as a result of which we have a proposal from Renshaw (Chapter 2) which is for a curriculum focusing on 'Human Movement Studies'. These historical and philosophical perspectives lead to a consideration of the curriculum planning process at the centre of which is the teacher; and Almond (Chapter 4), drawing on the findings of curriculum approaches in other subjects, reviews the options open to the physical educationist. In Chapter 5 he goes on to make recommendations for physical education as an element of an integrated studies curriculum, giving as his opinion that 'physical education departments cannot continue to retain a separate identity'.

The problems and opportunities in planning for curriculum renewal may realistically be assessed only when the facts concerning current practices and procedures are known and understood. Chapter 5 gives a detailed interpretation of the recently published Schools Council Inquiry into physical education in secondary schools and gives some consideration to the social context of the findings, especially with respect to the concept of 'open-v-closed'.

Examples of on-going innovatory practices are discussed in Chapter 6 by Gibbon who aligns himself emphatically with 'applied curriculum development hammered out in the school situation'. In the final chapter, Whitehead presents an effective commentary and summary of the forces—within the school and outside it—which shape the curriculum.

The authors, it will be noticed, are not fully in agreement with one another even on such important issues as the planning and teaching of the curriculum. To this extent the book is a fair reflection of the state of curriculum theory and development where healthy controversy abounds, and in the last analysis it is the teacher who must shape a satisfactory and appropriate working plan which he can operate— whether such a plan has, as its starting point, the statement of objectives or the identification of relevant 'issues'. In

general the authors have avoided prescriptions and the
reader will look in vain for 'hints and tips' on teaching
content and methods. The purpose is rather to take the
physical education teacher through the current controver-
sies, debates and speculations about curriculum renewal in
order to provide the background for an informed participation in the great wave of rethinking, experimenting and
reshaping to which present curricula are certain to be subjected in the next decade.

In 1969 Ann Jewett set herself the task (in a paper to the
AAHPER Convention, Boston) of predicting the shape of
the USA high school physical education programme in
1975. Six quotations from her description of the curriculum
at Would-you-Believe High School to which she had conveniently transported herself give the flavour of her predictions
and hopes:

(a) 'The emphasis is on the pod—or modular construction—with simple basic units easily convertible to
teaching stations of varying shapes and sizes.'

(b) 'Our students have access to the Instructional
Materials Center which is equipped with facilities for
viewing films and videotapes, carels for independent
study assisted by teaching machines and a growing
collection of books, charts, slides, films, recording and
learning programs selected or developed by members
of the physical education staff.'

(c) 'The planning committee includes students and parents.'

(d) 'All students are individually programmed.'

(e) 'We place a high premium on the aesthetic aspects of
movement experience, on expressive application of
movement abilities and on creative solutions to
movement problems.'

(f) 'We try to refine concepts of bio-mechanics and exercise physiology through experiences ... in sports
activities and training challenges.'

These kinds of predictions may have sounded strange in
1969, but today, while it may be impossible to point to a

particular school in Britain or the USA incorporating all these or similar ideas, it is no longer difficult to point to schools where one or more of these practices is being used successfully. It is clear that we are at the beginning of an exciting and challenging advance. What we need are knowledgeable, creative and courageous teachers who are given some freedom to experiment and innovate. Such educators confronting reality with their students will ensure a dynamic programme of renewal for physical education.

J. E. Kane
Loughborough, September 1975

The Curriculum of Physical Education—An Historical Perspective

Peter C. McIntosh

The Shorter Oxford Dictionary defines curriculum as 'A course: spec. a regular course of study as at a school or (Scottish) university'. It will not be appropriate to discuss here the special use of the term by Scottish universities, but the implications of 'a regular course of study' do need closer examination. A great deal of the physical education of children and adults has always taken place without the aid of any course of study. The development of locomotion for instance will take place in children in almost all human environments, even within the confines of a flat in a tower block. The acquisition of the skills of locomotion are so closely associated with the normal maturation of the individual that it often seems that no special measures are needed to educate children to crawl, stand, walk, run, hop and jump. Many other skills are likewise acquired by children on their own initiative through solitary play, street and field games, imaginative activity or rhythmic movement. In some environments children learn to swim without any formal instruction. In some they may develop climbing skills to an advanced standard. In this respect many physical skills differ from the mental skills associated with reading, writing and arithmetic in which development will cease, if it begins at all, at quite a low level unless there is some instruction and even perhaps a regular course of study. It is hardly surprising, therefore, that in the history of education many curricula have been devised which have not included any physical education.

Extra-curricular physical education

During the twelfth and thirteenth centuries there was a considerable expansion of education throughout Europe but there is no evidence that the curricula of the monastic schools and universities included any physical education. As late as 1560 the *Consuetudinarium Scholae Etonensis* laid down a curriculum and a timetable for boys at Eton College. The day began at 5 am with *Surgite* and continued with learning and repetition of learned passages of classic authors until prayers and bedtime at 8 pm. There were breaks for breakfast, dinner and supper and between 3 and 4 pm an hour's 'play time'. This must surely have been used by the boys for extra-curricular physical education (Maxwell Lyte, 1875, Chap. VII).

Elsewhere in Europe, the demand for formal physical education—a demand which stemmed from the economic and cultural renaissance—had led to the devising of courses of study in practical accomplishments. These courses, however, were not included in the curricula of schools, colleges and universities, not even Scottish universities, but were either incorporated in the teaching given at the courts of noblemen to aspiring courtiers or led to the establishment of institutions specifically for physical education. Vittorino da Feltre at the court of Mantua and Guarino da Verona at Ferrara are two notable Renaissance teachers who included physical education in their courses. In Florence, at least two schools existed in the fifteenth century for the teaching of physical skills and accomplishments, especially dancing and fencing, which were considered a necessary part of the education of *l'uomo universale*, the whole man. Similarly in England the education of scholars came to be distinct from the education of gentlemen. While the former contained within its curricula no physical education, the latter paid great attention to social accomplishments including the physical skills of dancing and combat for which courses of instruction were provided. Nor were courses confined to social accomplishments for the sake of status or prestige. When James Figg opened his school for 'Ye Noble Science of Defence' (or the 'Academie of Boxing' as it was sometimes called) at the 'Adam & Eve' in Tottenham Court Road in 1718, the purpose was to equip young bucks with the necessary skills to protect themselves in the unruly and sometimes riotous streets of London.

Importance attached by society or by a section of society to physical education has not always led to its inclusion in the curricula of schools or to the setting up of special schools. In the nineteenth century, with the growth of athleticism in middle and upper classes in Britain, enormous importance was attached to physical education in the form of organised sport, especially team games (football and cricket were the most popular) and rowing. A great deal of time was consequently devoted to these activities. At Rugby and Winchester in mid-century, boys spent three hours a day at cricket, for six days a week; at Eton the figures were higher still (*Report of Public Schools* (*Clarendon*) *Commission*, 1864, p. 97). Furthermore participation in games was compulsory. The compulsion, however, was imposed by the older boys on the rest, not by the teachers. There was, in the second half of the century, some coaching of games by masters and, in cricket, by 'professionals' employed for the purpose; but neither games nor any other form of physical education appeared on the timetable or in the curricula of the Public Schools. This situation continued well into the twentieth century. Not until the 1920s did the curricula of these schools make any provision for physical education. A similar situation obtained for music. Both these branches of education were treated as extra-curricular. This is not to say that all physical exercise was totally excluded from the programme imposed on boys by teachers. Physical drill was commonly used as punishment for petty offences. Again in some schools the whole population, or a large section of it, might be required to go through some routine exercises in mass formation for a few minutes before the beginning of morning lessons; and, of course, some physical training or drill was often associated with the activities of the Officers Training Corps which were organised by most Public Schools, but none of these features of the schools could be said to amount to the inclusion of physical education in the curriculum.

This view that games and sports, even when instruction was given, were properly outside the curriculum continued to affect the curricula of all schools long after the time when in state schools some form of drill or gymnastic exercise had been included in the curriculum. So it was that the Royal Commission on Physical Training in Scotland reported in 1903 that 'the organised game is a characteristically British institution ... but the bulk of the school population has never had the advantage of this institution ... the solution is cooperation with clubs and voluntary organisations for coaching and facilities' (Report, par. 181). One reason given for the exclusion of games from the curriculum was that weaker children would not be able to play and would, so to speak, go to the wall. Next year, in 1904, the Inter-Departmental Committee on Physical Deterioration, while endorsing the proposal that physical training should be universal, stated that 'no scheme of games alone can ever be made general enough to supply the place of methodical physical training' (see Report, par. 423) and recommended that games should be provided for children by voluntary agencies using public facilities. A continuous thread in the history of the curriculum in Britain has been a widespread view that activities which boys and girls would do, and indeed have done, in very large measure on their own initiative and in their free time should not be a subject for a regular course within the curriculum. This attitude may well largely account for the facts that physical education in the form of gymnastics found its place in the curriculum, as we shall see, long before more spontaneous forms of exercise, and that the gymnastics itself was so systematised that no child would have devised it or done it for its own sake.

Militarism and physical education

Before tracing the development of physical education in the curriculum in Britain since the middle of the nineteenth century one further general point must be made. Military needs have always been an influence in the history of physical education. In communities which were defended by a *citizen* army, such as the Greek city-states of the fifth century BC, military needs shaped the educational curriculum of the normal citizen. In some states these needs were paramount —as at Sparta; and although for a time Spartans won more victories than citizens of other states in the Olympic Games, which were essentially non-military in character, these successes were of secondary importance to military prowess. Even in Athens, where aesthetic considerations were of greater significance, the military need for physical education, especially during the Peloponnesian War, was far from unimportant. In communities such as the Roman Empire, which depended on a *professional* army and navy, the military form of physical education tended to be confined to institutions for military training while the education of the rest of the population was determined by other factors. The curriculum in such communities might or might not have included physical education; in the city of Rome in the first century AD school curricula did not include it. Even when direct military training has not formed part of schools' programmes, military needs and military practices *outside* the schools may well have been an indirect influence upon the curriculum. Two instances of this indirect influence are, firstly, the effect upon physical education in schools in the United States of congressional investigations which showed that in 1959, to meet a crisis in Europe, the government had to call up 755,000 men in order to recruit 196,000 fit soldiers; and, secondly, the effect on physical education in British Schools of commando training developed in the army schools of physical training during World War II. This particular effect upon the curriculum will be dealt with later.

1850–1900 Physical education takes root in the curriculum

In the middle of the nineteenth century in Britain there was no physical education in the curricula of schools whether these were the independent Public Schools or the elementary schools provided from public or voluntary funds. It is true that the first government department to have responsibility for education, a committee of the Privy Council set up in 1839, stated in its first report: 'The physical training of the children may therefore be usefully provided for on other grounds than its tendency to develop the muscular powers and to render the scholars robust and vigorous'. However, instead of advocating the inclusion of physical education in the curriculum, it went on to say that 'The physical exercises of the playground extend the moral influence of the teacher by encouraging the children to remain under his care *during the hours of recreation*' (Minutes of Committee of Council on Education 1839–40, p. 19). The report thus placed physical education unequivocally outside the curriculum.

It has to be recognised that the fact that a subject was useful did not at that time justify its place in the curriculum. In 1862 Lord Elcho introduced a motion in the House of Commons for the extension of the practice of systematised gymnastic training as well as military drill which had already been included in the curricula of schools for orphans and destitute children. He was answered by Mr Lowe on behalf of the government who said that Lord Elcho's proposal embodied an idea which he had to repudiate altogether—'the idea that it was the duty of the Privy Council to devise means, in addition to the existing grant, to promote the teaching of anything because it might be deemed useful' (*Hansard*, 1862).

Physical Education suffered from a disadvantage similar to that impeding scientific education. 'It was pointless to argue in the nineteenth century that science must be taught because it is vocationally useful (though this is what Spencer argued) since most people in schools and universities did not believe that professional training was the purpose of education. The subjects that were included in the curriculum were justified as being "right" or "sound"' (Brock, 1971). The most powerful pressure group for the inclusion of experimental or heuristic science in the curriculum was the X-Club, a group of nine men who met and dined regularly each month in London. It is interesting that two members of this club were also protagonists for the inclusion of physical education in the curriculum. They were Herbert Spencer, a philosopher and the author of *Education: Intellectual, Moral and Physical* (1859), and Thomas Huxley, whose reputation as a biologist was very high indeed.

Herbert Spencer was particularly concerned at the omission of physical education from the upbringing of girls; but he applied many of his remarks to boys' education and quoted the timetable of a training college for men teachers to show that between rising at 6 am and going to bed at 10 pm there was no provision for any exercise except a walk—which often was not taken. In general the curricula of schools in the middle of the century included no physical education. In the independent Public Schools extra-curricular physical education, largely restricted to team games and rowing, was very important and time-consuming. In elementary schools extra-curricular activities if they occurred at all took the form of military drill, of free-standing gymnastic exercises, and of playground games which were occasionally supervised by a teacher. Such physical education however was spasmodic.

The Forster Education Bill and the revised code of regulations

When the government brought in an Education Bill in 1870 the minister, W. E. Forster, received a strong plea from Matthias Roth to put physical education on a par with reading, writing and arithmetic (Roth, 1870). This he ignored. The revised code of regulations, issued after the Education Bill became law, gave a curriculum for children over seven years of age; its compulsory elements were reading, writing and arithmetic, with plain needlework for girls. Optional subjects were to be geography, history, grammar, algebra, geometry, natural philosophy, physical geography, natural science, political economy, languages or any definite subject of instruction extending over the classes to be examined in standards four, five and six (May 1971, p. 104).

The way was therefore open for one or more of the school boards, which the Act established covering the whole country, to introduce physical education. The School Board for London did just this.

The revised code of regulations also made it possible for attendance at drill under a competent instructor to be counted as school attendance for purposes of financial grant from the government. To implement this provision the Education Department made arrangements with the War Office for instruction by drill sergeants at the rate of sixpence a day and a penny a mile marching money. The exercises were to be taken from the War Office's *Field Exercise Book*. So, for boys, military drill became part of the curriculum. The School Board for London appointed Regimental Major William Sheffield as Drill Master and recommended to the Education Department in 1872 that the next year's code of regulations should permit similar provision for girls. The Department replied that the drill referred to was systematic military drill and therefore unsuitable for girls. Nevertheless the instructor employed by the Board did in fact drill 4922 girls in 1873. Both the girls and their mistresses were said to be highly appreciative.

The School Board for London took its duties seriously and in February 1871 set up a committee of fourteen to advise upon the curriculum. The chairman was Professor T. H. Huxley and the committee included Lord Sandon who in the next Conservative government became the minister responsible for education. In taking evidence the committee met the attitude that physical education should be extra-curricular. Mr Halifax from Dockhead School said that no methodical physical exercise was practised; the boys could be trusted to get that outside (May 1971). Nevertheless the Huxley Committee in its report of 13 June 1871 said: 'We recommend that music and drill be taught in every school during the period devoted to actual instruction. For infants, singing and physical exercises are of paramount importance' (May 1971, p. 93). A rudimentary form of physical education was thus included among essential subjects rather than discretionary subjects.

At first the drill was essentially military in character. Classes for men teachers included even bayonet exercises and skirmishing in open order. Her Majesty's inspector for the City of London reported: 'The boys are trained in exactly the same way as our own volunteers, much to their benefit as well as enjoyment' (Morrell, 1871). He believed that the general adoption of such training would lead to health and physical development, good habits of obeying orders and aptitude for military service.

The development of the curriculum of physical education under the School Board for London from 1870 to 1904 was significant and is well documented (May 1971, Chap. VII). Spalding, in assessing the work of the Board, claims that its decisions not only affected London but guided decisions of school boards in other areas (p. 31). The course of events in London may therefore indicate what was happening or was to happen elsewhere. The final report of the School Board for London claimed a four-fold advance for physical education: firstly in the range of free-standing exercises; secondly in exercises with apparatus—from simple wands to more sophisticated work in a fully equipped gymnasium under a qualified superintendent; thirdly in swimming instruction; and lastly in both the games of the playground (in, and out, of school hours) and the voluntary clubs for cricket and football (Report, 1870–1904, p. 115).

Military drill v gymnastic exercises

The initial attempt of the Board to introduce free-standing exercises of an exclusively military character met with two objections. First both in meetings of the Board and in Parliament there were objections to militarism. In 1875 the Board debated a motion that 'reviews or inspections of boys in military fashion tend to create a passion for what is called "glory", pernicious in its consequences to thousands by diverting their thoughts and aspirations from honourable and useful labour to a life of idleness and all its terrible concomitants, dreaded as a plague by parents'. The motion was lost by three votes to twelve. Next year there were petitions from a number of organisations including the Ratepayers to exclude the military element from drill. No immediate action was taken. In Parliament in 1875 two motions were debated calling for the introduction of gymnastic exercises into elementary schools in preference to or in addition to military drill. Viscount Sandon for the government expressed the belief that the introduction of military drill would be attended by very advantageous results and he could promise no further action.

The second objection was to girls doing military drill with no alternative being provided. In 1876 the Board resolved 'that instruction of girls in physical exercises in the school room and by, or under the eye of, the principal school mistress may be provided for the two hours secular instruction required by the New Code' (Minutes, 1876). Later in the year participation was made compulsory. Although these exercises were to be inspected by the Board's drill instructor, this resolution marked the introduction of a form of physical education other than military drill. It was also the first step in developing separate curricula for boys and for girls. Two years later the Board, under the influence of Matthias Roth, resolved to introduce Swedish gymnastics into all girls schools and departments. Miss Concordia Löfving who had qualified at the Royal Central Gymnastic Institute in Stockholm was appointed lady superintendent of physical exercises. While boys continued to do military drill, girls now had a syllabus based upon the following categories of exercise:

Introductory Exercises.
Spanbendings.
Heaving Movements.
Balance Movements.
Shoulder Exercises.
Abdominal Exercises.
Lateral Trunk Movements.
Jumping and Vaulting (marching and running).

Movements Producing Passive Extension of Muscles of the Legs.
Respiratory Exercises. (Österberg, 1885)

Controversy over the curriculum now polarised between military drill and the Swedish system. Miss Löfving's re-appointment was opposed in the Board in 1880 and 1881. So was the appointment of her successor Miss Martina Bergman in 1881. Even when it became clear that the Swedish system had much to offer to boys as well as to girls, the Board would only agree to permit it in 1883, 'care being taken that the military drill required by the New Code of the Education Department be not interfered with' (Minutes, 1883). To further the cause Lord Brabazon offered to pay the salary of a male instructor from Sweden and Captain Haasum was brought over in 1884.

The English system v the Swedish system

The death of Regimental Major Sheffield in 1888 provided an occasion for reorganisation. Dr Allan Broman from Sweden was appointed to develop the Swedish system and Thomas Chesterton was appointed to superintend the so-called English system which, he claimed, combined the best elements from all the Continental systems. At first both systems were taught as alternatives in addition to military drill for boys. Gradually Chesterton's system replaced Broman's system and after two years Allan Broman was not reappointed. Chesterton asserted that his system, although combined with drill, was not preparatory military training but was primarily designed to counteract the effects of school life. Meanwhile girls continued to have the Swedish system promoted by the Lady Organising Tutor, Miss E. Knighton. A comparison between the two classifications of exercise does not reveal a vast difference of content whatever may have been the differences in teaching method.

This dichotomy within the curriculum persisted for the rest of the century. In 1890 the government 'recognised' physical exercise as well as drill and in 1895 the Education

Mr Chesterton's Classification	Miss Knighton's Classification
Commencing position of upper and lower limbs	Preparatory Movements
Head Movements	Leg Movements
Arms raising and swinging	Dorsal Movements
Arms bending and stretching	Arm Extensions
Trunk Movements	Balance Movements
Trunk and Arm Movements	Shoulder Blade Movements
Leg and Hip Movements	Abdominal Movements
Side Lungeing	Lateral Bendings
Side Lungeing with Arm Movements	Leaping
Direct Lungeing with Arm Movements	Respiratory Movements
Balance Movements	
Shoulder Movements	
Exercises on the March	
Marching in Various Formations	
Figure Marching	

Department specifically commended the Swedish system along with 'Other drill or suitable physical exercises' (Report, 1893, p. 33). By 1900 the School Board for London had not only made inclusion of physical exercises in the timetable obligatory, it had specified three twenty-minute lessons a week for boys and girls and five fifteen-minute lessons for infants. In Birmingham a similar and parallel development of an indigenous system took place under the Superintendent Teacher of Physical Exercises, Samuel Bott. Manchester, Liverpool, Bristol and others of the larger school boards followed the example of Birmingham and London, but Leeds introduced the Swedish system in 1883.

Exercises with apparatus

The development of exercises with apparatus was much less extensive than that of free-standing exercises but an experimental gymnasium was opened at Crampton Street School, London in 1883 under Miss Bergman and Captain Haasum. It attracted from 200 to 300 visits in a single day. The *Daily News* reported a demonstration thus:

> The girls exercised first. They were dressed in blue serge tunics and knickerbockers with light blue sashes round their waists and were first put through ordinary callisthenic exercises by Miss Bergman who has a peculiarly sharp and businesslike manner in giving the word of

command. They climbed loose ropes and poles hanging from the roof, jumped from a spring board and exercised themselves upon what one must call a horizontal bar. One portion of the apparatus deserves brief notice, as it is quite unlike anything we have seen here. It consists of a large framework of wood cut into squares like the framework of a window. At the word of command, three or four girls swarmed up the structure like cats, and proceeded to wriggle themselves in and out of openings with grace and ease ... The boys were no less successful in their exercises which to some extent were a repetition of those by girls (May, 1971, p. 129).

However, the development of gymnastics on apparatus was hampered in two ways. The government's *Rules to be Observed in Planning and Fitting up Schools* stated even as late as 1902: 'since fixed gymnastic apparatus is unsuitable for children under fourteen years of age, a separate gymnasium is not required and cannot be approved' (Board of Education, 1902). In 1891 London's School Management Committee ruled out the use of apparatus in playgrounds as dangerous. During the nineties items such as parallel bars, horizontal beams, and horizontal ladders which had already been installed were removed from school playgrounds. Nevertheless some progress was made especially in higher-grade schools where gymnasia were provided for both boys and girls and physical education was required on the time-table.

Swimming

As early as 1872, the School Board of London wished to include swimming in the curriculum and asked the Education Department to allow the provision of baths and the employment of swimming instructors for purposes of grant. The Department refused and not until 1890 did it give assent to swimming to be provided in this way. However, London and Birmingham and other boards made their own arrangements for extra-curricular swimming at cheap rates. By 1880, 25,000 cheap tickets were being issued to school pupils in Birmingham (Molyneux, 1957, p. 216). From 1890 swimming was included in the curriculum in many cities. London built four swimming pools to cater for this subject and claimed that, between 1894 and 1896, 12,000 children had been taught to swim. By 1900 more than 30,000 school children in London were receiving instruction (Education Department, 1898). Swimming competitions continued to be organised by teachers outside the curriculum. Life-saving and land drill, however, came within it.

Games

Games, especially team games, were first introduced as extra-curricular activities by enthusiastic teachers. These teachers formed school sports associations to promote the games. The South London Schools Football Association founded in 1885 was the first schools sports association ever. The Birmingham Athletic Institute was also very active in promoting a number of games and sports but it was not until 1900 that the newly constituted Board of Education allowed games to be included in the curriculum. Even then they were regarded as merely supplementary physical education. The revised code of 1900 reviewed the scene in these words:

> Instruction in Swedish or other drill or in suitable physical exercises is a condition for the higher grant for discipline and organisation. Military drill for boys has been found very attractive in some districts and deserves encouragement. A healthy game which is one of the best forms of physical exercise will satisfy the conditions of the Code. In country schools such games are almost always possible, and if played during an attendance should be supervised by some member of the staff who should teach the most skilful method of play, and should encourage orderly behaviour and stop quarrelling. In most town schools, however, even in those which possess large play yards, such games are impossible, or possible for only a few scholars.
> The physical development of the frames of growing boys and girls imperatively requires, therefore, in such cases, some form of drill or gymnastics, and it becomes incumbent on teachers to make themselves familiar with those exercises that are best suited to develop a healthy frame without undue strain upon the scholar (Board of Education, 1900, par. 29).

There are two postscripts to the curriculum in the nineteenth century. First is that dancing was approved by Her Majesty's Inspectors in twenty schools in London in the latter years of the century but was dropped in 1901 after Sir John Gorst had said in the House of Commons that dancing was quite unsuitable for grant-earning purposes. The second postscript concerns girls' independent Public Schools. In a number of them, games, gymnastics, swimming and even dancing had been welded into a curriculum by teachers trained at Dartford College of Physical Training which had been established by Miss Bergman (later Mrs Bergman Österberg) in 1885. Notwithstanding the considerable and significant development of the curriculum in boards' schools the most advanced pioneers were in public and high schools for girls.

1900–1944 The Swedish system

Specialist colleges for women and colleges for women teachers provided the backbone of curriculum consolidation during the first thirty years of the twentieth century. Men pioneers, notably F. H. Grenfell, R. E. Roper and B. T. Coote, appeared early on the scene, having been to Sweden for their professional training; but the Swedish system which was to be the solid core of the curriculum until World War II rested upon foundations laid by Mrs Bergman Österberg and her former pupils. Indeed, but for them it might not have survived the shocks of the Boer War. These shocks included not only defeats at the hands of Boer farmers who failed to observe the conventions of warfare, but also the wholesale rejection of recruits for the army. In Manchester in 1899, 8000 were rejected from a total of only 12,000 volunteers and no more than 1200 were accepted as fit in all respects. There was an immediate demand for military training in schools and to meet it the Board of Education issued the *Model Course of Physical Training for use in the Upper Departments of Elementary Schools*, based largely upon a handbook issued by the War Office, *Infantry Training 1902*.

This publication was a retreat from the Swedish system and was met with protests from Members of Parliament, the National Union of Teachers, the Medical Profession and many interested organisations. An interdepartmental committee was therefore set up to examine the Model Course and in 1904 pronounced it unsatisfactory because there were no underlying 'general principles educed from a consideration of the function of physical exercise in a well-ordered course of general education for children' (Report, 1904, col. 203). The report included a syllabus which did a little to demilitarise physical education but also ruled out the use of dumb-bells, weights and music during the initial learning of exercises.

Unfortunately for the Swedish system the government had already appointed Colonel G. Malcolm Fox to be Inspector of Physical Training and he in turn had secured the appointment of peripatetic instructors from the army. Their influence persisted and was more difficult to counter than that of the Model Course. However, Miss Roberts, later Mrs Impey, a former student of Dartford, produced in 1905 a *Handbook of Free Standing Gymnastics* which was written 'with the idea of providing the Elementary teacher, already engaged in giving "drill" lessons, with a series of complete lessons on the lines of the Model Course'. Part 11 gave 'a theoretical equivalent to the course of practical instruction' (Impey, 1905).

The influence of Miss Roberts' handbook upon the curriculum was considerable. The preface to the second edition states disingenuously: 'a comparison of this Handbook with the syllabus of Physical Exercises issued by the Board of Education in 1904, showed some more or less important differences. The official 1908 edition, however, shows conformity to the Handbook in so many of these points that some justification is required for republication of the latter' (Impey, 1915). The adoption of Miss Roberts' work by the government represented a triumph for the Swedish system, but failure to acknowledge the source of material was resented and almost led to legal action.

The appointment in 1908 of the first woman, Miss L. M.

Rendell, as His Majesty's Inspector to supervise physical exercises, and in 1909 of F. H. Grenfell as Inspector of Physical Training assured a Swedish basis for the curriculum so far as it depended upon advice from the government. Furthermore the establishment of a medical department of the Board of Education in 1908 under Dr (later Sir) George Newman with oversight of physical training in schools gave a therapeutic orientation to this advice. Nevertheless examination of the 1909 Syllabus shows the persistance of military precision and drill formations.

Field games in the elementary school curriculum

The syllabus of 1909 provided seventy-one tables of exercises but devoted only a few paragraphs to games and these were traditional street and playground games such as 'Fox and Geese'. No guidance was given on team games—which had not made much progress in the curriculum. The code of 1900 allowed playground games in the curriculum but a new clause issued in 1906 was required before field games could be included. Thereafter organised games—cricket, hockey and football for boys and similar suitable games for girls— were officially allowed in school time. This represented an attempt to introduce into the curriculum of elementary schools what had long been an important feature of extra-curricular activity in Public Schools. The originators of the new clause were the President of the Board of Education, Augustine Birrell, two of His Majesty's Inspectors, E. G. A. Holmes and A. P. Graves, and the permanent secretary to the Board, Robert Morant, who had been a boy at Winchester. The 1906 clause was a decision of great importance for the curriculum. Hitherto the purposes of the curriculum had been to promote organic and functional physical development and to inculcate habits of discipline and cleanliness. These objectives in 1906 needed no more than the syllabuses of physical exercises, Swedish, British or what you will. The introduction of games was the introduction of a new objective for the curriculum: to provide for moral and social education. It had been expressed by Morant in his preface to the New Code for 1904:

> The purpose of the Public Elementary School is to form and strengthen the character and to develop the intelligence of the children entrusted to it, and to make the best use of the school years available in assisting both boys and girls according to their different needs to fit themselves, practically as well as intellectually, for the work of life ... The school must afford them every opportunity for the development of their bodies, not only by training them in appropriate physical exercises and in encouraging them in organised games but also by instructing them in some of the simpler laws of health ... The corporate life of the school, especially in the playground, should develop that instinct for fair play and for loyalty to one another which is the germ of a wider sense of honour in later life (Code, 1904).

The Fisher Education Act of 1918

The development of the curriculum whether in gymnastics or in games was dependent upon the adequacy of teachers and of facilities. In 1909 physical training was made a compulsory and examinable subject in all teachers' training colleges. Some eighty colleges turning out 5000 teachers a year were involved. A few courses for men specialist-teachers were started but compared with the flourishing colleges for women specialists the provision for men was negligible. Facilities were the subject of a series of circulars and advice from the government, but the significant advance was made in the Fisher Education Act of 1918 which, in clause 17, allowed local education authorities to provide all manner of facilities for gymnastics, games, swimming, camping and other forms of social and physical training.

The scene was now set for curriculum development along several lines. In elementary schools free-standing exercises of Swedish type, playground games, swimming and some field games (where facilities existed) became part of the curriculum. In secondary schools came Swedish gymnastics with fixed and portable apparatus in fully equipped gymnasia, swimming, and a limited range of team games (football and cricket for boys; hockey, netball, rounders and tennis for girls). There were occasional experiments both in curriculum content and teaching method. Before moving on it should be noted that during the war of 1914–18 no serious attempt was made to remilitarise the curriculum. Physical education was by then protected by its close supervision by the medical department of the Board.

The development of physical education in elementary schools was encouraged from the centre by the issue in 1919 of a Syllabus of Physical Training for Schools to replace the 1909 Syllabus of Physical exercises. In the new syllabus the approach was much less formal, although far from free or informal judged by the criteria of the 1970s. The buildings, however, did not include gymnasia and their multipurpose halls contained few if any pieces of portable gymnastic apparatus. Hoops, canes, skittles, bean bags, coloured braids and some balls were the kind of apparatus to be found in schools for those who were going to leave school at fourteen years of age. For pupils who entered secondary schools at nine, ten or eleven with a view to full-time education until sixteen or beyond, the facilities and consequently the gymnastic curriculum were different. Many grammar schools built from 1902 onwards had gymnasia equipped with a full range of Swedish apparatus: climbing ropes, double beams, wall bars, window ladders, vaulting boxes, benches and agility mats. In such schools there was a highly developed gymnastic curriculum under the control of specialist or semi-specialist teachers.

The Hadow Report and after

After the appearance of the Hadow Report, *The Education of the Adolescent* in 1926, secondary education was slowly reorganised so that all children at eleven years of age had a break in their school life and either proceeded to grammar schools or to senior elementary schools or classes. A new syllabus of physical training appeared in 1933 with two parts, one for use in junior schools for children under eleven and a second for use in senior schools. Schools however could not be rebuilt at once and the gymnastics offered in senior elementary schools could not approach that of grammar schools. Portable vaulting and agility apparatus was provided and curricula therefore differed according to whether fixed and portable apparatus was available or portable apparatus only. The keynote to the gymnastic curriculum, with or without apparatus, was 'posture'. In 1932 the medical department of the Board dogmatically stated:

> The ultimate criterion of the success of any scheme or system of physical training is the carriage, mobility and equilibrium of the human body. If there is one test of the strength, tone and balance of the body it is posture, for this depends on the coordination of the muscles acting on the skeleton. Good posture indicates health and soundness; bad posture the reverse (Report, 1932, p. 81).

Physiological dogma was also used to judge other parts of the curriculum. Crawl swimming was condemned by the chief medical officer because it was 'not so correct physiologically as the breast stroke' (Report, 1926, p. 90).

Games make little progress in curriculum

Despite the far-sightedness of Augustine Birrell and his advisers in admitting games to the curriculum in 1906 and despite the legislative permission given to local education authorities in 1918 to provide facilities, little help or advice was given by the Board of Education. Of eleven publications on physical education issued by the Board between 1919 and 1927 only one, issued in 1920, was devoted to non-gymnastic activities. However, many local education authorities used their own initiative. In 1920 the Education Committee in London assumed full and direct financial responsibility for hiring playing-fields and swimming-baths for secondary schools. Birmingham Education Committee bought ground and provided playing-fields for 23,500 school children in 1924. By 1926 more than 90,000 children in Sheffield were being transported by tramcar each week to playing-fields. Participation by the pupils in many economically depressed areas was restricted by lack of boots and clothes as well as by shortage of pitches, but swimming was by 1930 well established and found a place in the curriculum of most schools where facilities were available.

1944–1973 'Movement'

When World War II broke out in 1939 the organisation and the content of the curriculum of physical education was disrupted. During the war the organisation was radically changed by the Education Act of 1944, and when the curriculum emerged afterwards the pattern was different. In discussing this period it will be apposite to look first at the government's publication of 1972, *Movement, Physical Education in the Primary Years*. Part 1 concerns 'movement'*, growth and learning. Part 2 has separate chapters on gymnastics, dance, games, swimming, athletics and outdoor activities, all of which were by that year accepted in the curriculum of physical education for primary as well as secondary schools. We have already traced the development up to 1939 of a curriculum of gymnastics with games and swimming. The table of contents of the 1972 publication reveals a great expansion of the curriculum and a new approach, the approach of 'movement'. In the post-war years, 'movement' replaced 'posture' as the key word and

---

* 'Movement' is a general term meaning 'change of position'. It has attracted particular meanings in the contexts of military affairs, horogogy, music, religion, politics, art and commerce. In the context of physical education its meaning has usually been restricted to human movement, that is, changing the position of the human body or its parts; but even within this compass the term has been used since the 1940s in a variety of restricted ways. 'Basic movement', 'art of movement', 'movement training', 'art and science of movement', 'movement education', 'human movement studies' are all terms which have been used. They all have the word 'movement' as a common element but the historian quickly discovers that the common word does not imply a common concept and that the restricting predicate has been the important and significant part of the term. If the term 'movement' or even 'human movement' is used by itself, it can have only its dictionary meaning and has no curricular or other special significance. The reader must therefore always consider the terms, wherever they appear in this book, in the context defined or implied by the user.

yardstick for judging the curriculum. It is not certain when
the term 'movement' was first used in this way or whence it
came, but it is possible to trace three main sources of the
new approach to physical education, each source largely
independent of the others.

The sources of the 'movement' approach

The first source was dance in Central Europe, although at
one time it might have been 'natural' gymnastics from the
same geographical area. In the later nineteenth century and
early twentieth century physical education in Germany was
strongly affected by a dispute between *'turners'* and devotees
of sport. By 1900 *turnen* had become formal and rigid
indoor gymnastics. *'Turners'* decried sport as un-German.
Those who espoused sport counter-attacked the *'turners'* and
went for prowess and records, especially after the appointment of Carl Diem as Secretary of the German Olympic
Committee in 1906. One result of the dispute was the emergence of a number of rhythmic-gymnastic schools led by
men who all shared a dislike of both sport and *turnen* but
who approached the situation from different starting points.
Bess Mensendieck's aims were hygienic and physiological;
Bode derived his ideas from the philosophers, Klages and
Palagyi, and called his system *'ausdrucks-gymnastik'* or
'expression-gymnastics'; von Laban was a dancer, founded
several dance schools, the first being in Munich in 1910, and
established a number of 'movement choirs'. Gaulhofer and
Margarete Streicher in Austria based their system of *'natür-
lisches turnen'*, natural gymnastics, on the observation of
children's own movement impulses and spontaneous play;
Jacques Dalcroze set up a college of eurythmics at Hellerau
and influenced Bode. Isadora Duncan visited Germany early
in the century and, according to Ted Shawn, gave the
Germans 'a new vision of vast possibilities within the art of
dance never before realised by them' (Shawn, 1954). She also
made an impact in Britain and inspired a number of
disciples, Ruby Ginner, Irene Mawer, Madge Atkinson and
Margaret Morris, to attempt the popularisation of the free

approach to dance. Accomplished exponents of this type of dance were Martha Graham and Charles Weidman.

By 1939 representatives of a number of these schools of rhythmic gymnastics or free dance had a tenuous foothold in Britain, but in the heyday of the Swedish system they made few inroads into the normal school curriculum. Dalcroze's eurythmics were taught at Dartford College of Physical Training in the early years of the century and probably made Swedish exercises more plastic and rhythmic. Laban's work was noticed in England in 1924. From 1934 until 1941 Kurt Joos, a student and disciple of Laban who founded the company Ballet Joos, taught at Dartington Hall in Devon. The Austrian gymnastics of Gaulhofer and Streicher were introduced at Chelsea College of Physical Education for the training of women teachers in 1924. Miss Odland who taught it died the next year and it lapsed but was reintroduced in 1932.

In 1933 the Liberal movements in Germany received a setback with the assumption of power by Adolf Hitler. The political suppression and persecution of individuals which followed this event caused a number of liberal reformers in physical education to seek asylum in Britain and to continue to develop their theories in the atmosphere of tolerance and (later) of encouragement which existed here. Among them were Rudolf von Laban and Lisa Ullman. Laban came in 1936 but concerned himself with dance and movement in industry rather than physical education. However, at about this time Leslie Burrows and Louise Soelberg who had studied under Mary Wigman—who in turn had been trained by Laban—set up the Dance Centre in London to promote modern dance under the name of Central European dance.

By 1939 an essential difference between the gymnasts and the dancers from Central Europe could have been detected. On the one hand Margarete Streicher, in an article in 1938 entitled 'The Principles of Human Movement', categorised movement under three headings:

(a) locomotion (walking, running, jumping, climbing, crawling, swimming, gliding, wriggling and so on);

(b) movements with objects ('The use of apparatus', she said, 'is indispensable to give children the possibility of enjoying the whole wealth of movements such as are available to all human beings living in the open air');
(c) educational movements or artificial movements (e.g. knee bending and stretching) (Streicher, 1938).

On the other hand Lucile Czarnowski, in an article, 'Dance and its Place in Physical Education', written in 1939, stated that there were no fixed rules or techniques which must be followed; the body was its own instrument and the expression 'movement', was idiomatic, not grammatic. 'The contemporary dance form', she wrote, 'affords an excellent physical and functional training of the whole body with an immediate goal and purpose for such training' (Czarnowski, 1939). The gymnasts, without by any means ignoring aesthetic criteria, were concerned with natural movement from a functional point of view. They considered small and large apparatus indispensable. The dancers who used only choreographic apparatus regarded 'movement' as primarily a mode of expression but claimed functional effects as well.

It was not only in the use of apparatus that the two groups differed but in the use of words and terminology. For instance, in her treatment of weight Margarete Streicher referred to gymnastics as a game with gravity; she went on to show how the laws of Newtonian physics applied to all human movement and how they must be understood and appreciated. Her use of the term 'equilibrium' was scientifically correct (Streicher, 1970). Ruth Morison, a post-war follower of Laban, stated that in Movement Education the weight factor of motion should not be confused with body weight. The weight factor related to control of energy output and to the effect which this had in producing different intensities of strength and lightness in movement. She even claimed that we have the ability to make ourselves light or strong or heavy or elastic—according to need (Morison, 1960). This is certainly not a scientifically acceptable use of terms or even of language. No one who thinks that 'light' is the opposite of 'strong' will score high in a verbal-reasoning test. Perhaps the advocates of 'expressive movement' were deceived by the very illusions which they sought to produce in spectators.

The distinction between modern dance and natural gymnastics is important because, when war broke out in 1939 and severed communication with Central Europe, the dancers were already present in Britain and the gymnasts were not. Dance won the day. At the Easter holiday course of the Ling Physical Education Association in 1940 Rudolph von Laban and Lisa Ullman demonstrated Central European dance. They made such an impact that the conference requested the Board of Education to promote Modern Dance in schools. From this point Laban attracted a large and enthusiastic following of women teachers, local authority organisers and inspectors. In 1946 the chief medical officer of the Ministry of Education recorded that experiments in Modern Dance, which had started in girls' schools during the war, were continuing on a larger scale in Manchester, Sheffield, Middlesbrough and many other centres. He commended its 'high value in developing feeling for and understanding of "movement"'. The term 'movement' and phrases incorporating it, such as 'art of movement', 'movement training', 'basic movement' and 'movement education' came to be used more and more in place of dance as those who championed the new cause extended their claims upon physical education (McIntosh, 1971).

The second source of inspiration came from a scheme of remedial gymnastics developed by Sophia Dudgeon in Halifax from 1926 onwards. Her innovations were in teaching method rather than in content. She trained children to work on their own without command, to watch each other under the gymnast's guidance and to discuss good and bad movement with the gymnast. She also was careful to choose exercises which children enjoyed and she gave them standards of attainment to aim for. Soon it became clear that children visiting Miss Dudgeon's clinic made more progress in physical competence than those who attended ordinary school classes. The organiser for boys' schools, A. Bilborough, then worked out with Sophia Dudgeon an approach to gymnastics which would put children in situations where each of them used his own initiative and found his own way of solving physical problems (Johnstone, 1973). Expansion of these ideas was checked by the war but they were developed in Halifax from 1947; and when Bilborough moved to Lancashire he worked with fellow organiser, Percy Jones, to spread the new approach far and wide through courses for teachers (especially men teachers), through a film and later in 1963, a book, *Physical Education in the Primary School*. Although they use the term 'movement', the curriculum innovations of Dudgeon, Bilborough and Jones, were essentially gymnastic rather than dance. They made their first impact on men teachers and in primary schools.

The third source of inspiration was the army, in particular the school of physical training at Northern Command. Here, in 1943 the annual conference of local authority organisers with some of His Majesty's Inspectors saw a demonstration of a new approach to physical training. The defeat of France and evacuation of Dunkirk had convinced many that a new approach to training was needed. Obstacle training became of supreme importance. All manner of obstacles, natural and contrived, were used to develop individual agility and fitness, as well as personal attitudes to achievement and endurance. The demonstration made an immediate impact on the educationists. Catherine Cooke, organiser of physical education in Bristol, was the first to put the army's ideas to the test in schools. In 1944 a net was erected over a pole, eight-feet high, in an infants' playground and parallel ropes were installed in the hall of a junior school. Other climbing apparatus was devised and improvised in many primary schools in Bristol and elsewhere. The variety and unknown potential of these pieces of apparatus demanded a new teaching technique. For a time it was the children who were showing the teachers what could be done. The appeal of personal and individual discovery of solutions to physical problems was strong to children and teachers. Formal groupings leading to class activities were gradually abandoned in favour of directions or suggestions which every child could interpret in his or her own way and according to his or her own capacity.

'Movement' and the curriculum

The blending of Laban's modern dance, Sophia Dudgeon's orthopaedic and remedial exercises and the army's obstacle training into a new curriculum of physical education for both primary and secondary schools took place between the end of the war and the publication of *Movement, Physical Education in the Primary Years* in 1972. An interim stage was reached when the Ministry of Education produced *Moving and Growing* in 1952 and *Planning the Programme* in 1953. The first volume listed fields of physical education such as games, swimming, 'movement' as an art, dance and 'PT', but the copious illustrations showed that the Ministry had given up the Swedish system even if it could not bring itself to abandon 'PT'. It clearly recognised the significance of the truth later enshrined in the Plowden Report of 1967 that 'finding out' is better than 'being told' and this applied to both functional and expressive movement (Central Advisory Committee for Education, 1967).

In secondary schools the situation was sharply divided between boys' departments and girls' departments. The women teachers who followed Laban received their first authoritative statements from him in *Effort* (1947) and *Modern Educational Dance* (1948). In these books he identified four factors of motion—weight, space, time and flow; eight basic combinations of weight, space and time—namely slashing, pressing, wringing, punching, gliding, flicking, dabbing and floating; and sixteen movement themes. He made some far-reaching claims such as: 'It is obvious that a person who has learnt to distinguish the feel of pressing and gliding in all their shades of intensity will be able to do the practical tasks in which transitions between these two efforts are involved incomparably better and easier than a person who has hitherto never experienced such feel consciously' (Laban, 1947). He also stated that those who had practised the eight basic actions would be able to choose the appropriate movements for any tasks which they faced. His devotees began to claim that modern educational dance and then the art of movement was fundamental to all physical education and that Laban's principles provided not merely a frame of analysis for all physical tasks but also a method of teaching every game and sport as well as dance and gymnastics. For a time 'movement' training usurped physical education in girls' schools and there were some very bizarre attempts to teach, for instance, swimming and even hockey through the medium of dance and mime.

Gradually common sense and some acquaintance with what had been discovered by psychologists about transfer of training prevailed. Differentiation within 'movement' education took place in the 1950s until timetables showed, distinctly, modern educational gymnastics and modern educational dance. Furthermore swimming and games and sports were recognised as having identifiable and specific skills which had to be learned as such. They were not just aspects of movement. As differentiation proceeded and gymnastic apparatus was used again, it became clear that Laban's dabbing, flicking and other six basic actions were not helpful in devising movement with the surviving Swedish apparatus. The four factors of weight, space, time and flow were retained as concepts and terms, but a whole new taxonomy of movement was devised for educational gymnastics in secondary schools.

Meanwhile men teachers strongly resisted the claims of 'movement' education and the personalities of some of its exponents. They were not disposed to accept aesthetic criteria as overriding in physical education. They persisted for a time with traditional Swedish gymnastics; but for older boys they adopted circuit training which, like 'movement' training and the new teaching in primary schools, allowed a tailor-made programme of exercise for each individual. Circuit training, which was devised for university students by Morgan and Adamson, was adopted widely in secondary schools (Morgan, 1957). In the sixties many men teachers adopted a form of modern educational gymnastics, but it stemmed more from Bilborough and Jones than from Laban whose terminology was often not used.

Games, sports and athletics

In boys' secondary schools after World War II, games, sports, track and field athletics and swimming gained ground within the curriculum. The same trend occurred in girls' schools but was less marked because of the emphasis on the 'art of movement'. The trend was made possible by the Education Act of 1944 which made it legally obligatory for local education authorities to provide facilities for physical education including games and sports. The Act also reorganised education so that all boys and girls over eleven years of age were to have secondary education; and the justification for two curricula—one for secondary pupils and one for senior elementary pupils—disappeared. Furthermore schools were more and more influenced by consumer demand in the courses which they offered. In physical education adolescent boys and girls were attracted to adult games, sports and recreations but not necessarily to the traditional team games and athletics. Combat sports and individual sports were particularly in demand; judo and badminton were especially popular but archery, squash rackets, golf, fencing, skating, horse-riding and other sports were also introduced into the curriculum. Introductory courses were provided at public expense because under the 1944 Act any subject included within the curriculum had to be at no cost to the pupil. In the 1970s the trend has been to introduce many of these games and sports at an earlier and earlier age. Children learn to swim at five years of age and may compete at seven. Children go skiing in school parties at ten. The inclusion of games, athletics and swimming in primary school curricula has received official encouragement from the Department of Education and Science in its 1972 handbook although it is made clear that adult forms of games and sports are rarely suitable for primary children without modification.

Outdoor activities

Outdoor activities enjoy a separate chapter in the handbook.

The inclusion of these in the curricula of secondary schools and, later of primary schools was a post-war development. The initial stimulus came from Germany. Some outdoor activities, especially camping, were developed by Baden-Powell and the Scout Movement from 1897; and camping was an activity encouraged by the Board of Education, so that by 1928 fifteen local education authorities were running camps for school children (Report, 1928, p. 38). But scouting and camping fell for the most part outside the curriculum. Kurt Hahn, however, a refugee like Laban from Nazi Germany, introduced what were called 'outward bound' activities into the curriculum of his school at Gordonstoun in Scotland. For a century team games had been viewed as a pre-eminent means of character training. Kurt Hahn now advocated expeditions and community service to develop initiative, courage, leadership and stamina as well as desirable social behaviour. The Outward Bound Movement captured the educational imagination at the same time and for the same reasons as obstacle training in the army. Many schools introduced outdoor activities on land and water into the curriculum, and by 1958 twenty-three had set up their own outdoor-activity centres. In the same year the Duke of Edinburgh, who had been a pupil at Kurt Hahn's school, launched his Award Scheme with an expedition section based on outdoor activities. He intended the scheme as a spare-time scheme but almost at once it was adopted by many schools to make their curricula more attractive and purposeful for their pupils. In addition to basic training in camping and expedition work, climbing, sailing and canoeing were introduced into the curricula of schools—even in such an unpromising environment as the metropolis of London.

In one hundred years from 1870 to 1970 the curriculum of physical education developed from simple military drill to a variegated and bewildering pattern of activities so that in any one school, primary or secondary, the actual curriculum depended upon the choice and qualifications of the physical education teachers:

It may seem that children's learning has been broken down into disconnected pieces, and that the topic has been physical education as an aggregate of separate elements rather than movement as a unifying concept. But the essential unity of education in movement stems from the curriculum established by the teacher and experienced by the children in their varied activity (Department of Education and Science, 1972, p. 119).

References

BOARD OF EDUCATION (1900) *Code of Regulations revised.* HMSO: London.

BOARD OF EDUCATION (1902) *Rules to be Observed in Planning and Fitting up Public Elementary Schools.* HMSO: London.

BOARD OF EDUCATION (1926) Report of the Chief Medical Officer. HMSO: London.

BOARD OF EDUCATION (1928) Report of the Chief Medical Officer of the Ministry of Education. HMSO: London.

BOARD OF EDUCATION (1932) Report of the Chief Medical Officer. HMSO: London.

BROCK, W. H. (1971) 'Prologue to heurism' in *The Changing Curriculum.* History of Education Society: London.

Code of Regulations for Elementary Schools (1904) in MCINTOSH, P. C. (1968) *Physical Education in England since 1800.* G. Bell: London, p. 146.

CZARNOWSKI, L. (1939) 'Dance and its place in Physical Education'. *Journal of Physical Education,* **xxxi**, 200–208.

Daily News (7 July 1884) quoted in MAY, J. *op. cit.*

DEPARTMENT OF EDUCATION AND SCIENCE (1972) *Movement: Physical Education in the Primary Years.* HMSO: London.

Final Report of the School Board for London 1870–1904 (1904). London County Council: London, p. 115.

Hansard (1862) **168**, col. 22.

IMPEY, E. A. (1905) *A Handbook of Free-Standing Gymnastics.* Sherratt and Hughes: London.

IMPEY, E. A. (1916) *op. cit.*

JOHNSTONE, J. C. (1973) 'The influence of the movement approach on development in physical education in England'. MA thesis, University of Birmingham.

LABAN, R. VON (1947) *Effort* and (1948) *Modern Educational Dance*. Macdonald and Evans: London.

MAY, J. (1971) 'Curriculum development under the School Board for London: Physical Education'. MEd thesis, University of Leicester.

MAXWELL LYTE, H. C. (1875, 4th edn. 1911) *The History of Eton College*. Macmillan: London.

MCINTOSH, P. C. (1968) *Physical Education in England since 1800*. G. Bell: London.

MCINTOSH, P. C. (1971) 'The recent history of physical education in England with particular reference to the development of movement education' in *History of Physical Education and Sport*. Athletics Institute: Chicago.

'Minutes of the Committee of Council on Education 1839–40' in MCINTOSH, P. C. (1968) *op. cit.*, p. 88.

Minutes of the School Board for London (1876) 1, 2.

Minutes of the School Board for London (1883) 8, 11.

MORISON, R. (1960) *Educational Gymnastics for Secondary Schools*. R. Morison: Liverpool.

MORRELL, J. D. (1871) 'Reports of Her Majesty's Inspectors' in MAY, J. *op. cit.*, p. 112.

MOLYNEUX, D. D. (1957) 'The development of physical recreation in the Birmingham District 1871–1892'. Unpublished MA thesis, University of Birmingham.

MORGAN, R. E. and ADAMSON, G. (1957) *Circuit Training*. G. Bell: London.

'The New Code of Regulations 1871' in MAY, J. *op. cit.*

ÖSTERBERG, M. (1885) 'Synopsis of the Ling System' in MAY, J. *op. cit.*, p. 122.

Report of the Central Advisory Committee for Education (1967) (Plowden Report). *Children and their Primary Schools*. HMSO: London.

Report of the Education Department 1893–4. HMSO: London.

Report of Inter-Departmental Committee on Physical Deterioration (1904). HMSO: London.

Report of Inter-Departmental Committee on the Model Course of Physical Exercises (1904). HMSO: London.

Report of the Public Schools (Clarendon) Commission 1. HMSO: London.

Report of Royal Commission on Physical Training (Scotland) (1903). HMSO: London.

REYNOLDS, E. E. (1942) *Baden-Powell.* Oxford University Press: London, p. 137.

ROTH, M. D. (1870) *A Plea for the Compulsory Teaching of the Elements of Physical Education in our National Elementary Schools, or the claims of Physical Education to rank with reading, writing and arithmetic.* M. D. Roth: London. *passim.*

SHAWN, T. (1954, revised edn. 1968) *Every Little Movement.* Dance Horizons: New York.

SPALDING, T. A. (1900) *The Work of the London School Board.* London County Council: London.

STREICHER, M. (1938) 'The Principles of Human Movement'. *Journal of Physical Education,* xxx, 168–76.

STREICHER, M. (1970) in STRUTT, BETTY E. (ed.) *Reshaping Physical Education.* Manchester University Press: Manchester.

CHAPTER TWO

Human Movement Studies and the Curriculum

Peter Renshaw

Curriculum planning in schools and colleges is frequently bedevilled by the actions of unreflective pragmatists whose judgments are dominated by such factors as tradition, logistics, power, political expediency and economic constraints. In many cases demands for innovation result in a mild curricular face-lift, in which fundamental reform is sacrificed to those surface changes which will not threaten the *status quo*. Admittedly, any radical change will focus on both the formal and informal structure of the institution—on its administrative processes, its decision-making machinery and on its underlying culture—thus not limiting itself to aspects of the curriculum and teaching methods. Nevertheless, as the curriculum lies at the heart of the educational process, the teacher has a moral responsibility to continually reappraise the nature of those curricular activities for which he is concerned. The teacher of physical education is no exception. This is particularly the case at present as he is in the middle of a period of critical inquiry into the characteristics, rationale and status of his subject. This chapter intends to limit itself to one facet of the debate: a philosophical examination of Human Movement Studies with some possible implications for curricula in schools and colleges. As philosophy is concerned essentially with problems of meaning and justification, the argument will focus on a cluster of key questions. For instance, is Human Movement an autonomous discipline or is it more logical to view it as a field of knowledge drawing on several distinct forms of thought? If it fails to satisfy the conditions of a unitary mode of experience, is it possible to locate and to define some central distinguishing feature? What ways of knowing contribute to an understanding of human movement? How might these be characterised and in what way might they be related to each other? What constitutes the theoretical and practical study of Human Movement? What is the relationship between Human Movement Studies and Physical Education? How far can they both be considered to be of educational value? Such inescapably philosophical questions need to be asked if teachers are to clarify the logical status of their activity.

The nature of Human Movement Studies

Human Movement Studies might be described simply as those areas of study which illuminate our understanding of the phenomenon 'human movement'. It is now widely recognised that the many different facets of human movement can be described, analysed and explained adequately only through the medium of three fundamental modes of thought: through philosophy (e.g. aesthetics and philosophical psychology), the physical sciences (e.g. kinesiology and biomechanics) and the human sciences (e.g. psychology, social psychology, sociology, cultural anthropology and history) (Arnold, 1973, pp. 17–18; Curl, 1973, pp. 7–17; Hinks *et al.*, 1971, pp. 4–10; Mauldon, 1970, p. 16; Mawdsley, 1971, p. 43; Renshaw, 1972b, pp. 92–106; Webb, 1970, p. 3). On this view it can be maintained that Human Movement Studies is a 'field of knowledge' rather than a logically cohesive, autonomous discipline like mathematics or physics. The study of the myriad forms and functions of human movement does not depend on one distinctive mode of thinking or method of inquiry. Its knowledge is not organised around a single system of interlocking principles, concepts and definitions, designed to direct attention to a particular type of question or way of looking at the world. Rather, the events and phenomena associated with human movement can be understood only through several inter-related, yet distinctive, conceptual perspectives. Nevertheless, despite the importance of the inter-relationships between these contributory disciplines, this does not imply that the whole domain can be distinguished by a 'natural "organic" unity' as is claimed by Gordon Curl (1973, pp. 7–12). In contrasting Human Movement Studies with such themes as 'the neighbourhood', 'man and his environment' and 'rural studies', he argues that their unity is 'artificial' as distinct from the 'natural unity' of Movement Studies. But on closer examination it is difficult to see how the supposed unity of areas like Ecology, Medicine, Environmental Studies or Home Economics is more artificial than that claimed for Human Movement Studies. Many areas of human experience can be understood only through the medium of several symbolic systems. For instance, a balanced sex education might draw on biology, literature, psychology, ethics, religion and history. Or an understanding of the development of a particular society might place an essentially historical focus within a wider contextual framework through such disciplines as literature, science, religion, philosophy and the arts. In each case a multi-disciplinary approach is taken in order to facilitate the grasp of a specific area of interest. If the interconnections between the different perspectives are made explicit, it would seem that such fields of knowledge contain their own internal conceptual coherence rather than a 'natural' or 'artificial' unity.

Perhaps the most confusing point in Curl's (1973) account is his claim that the various forms of knowledge that contribute to an understanding of human movement 'converge and cohere in an organic fashion, in a mode analogous to the organism itself' (p. 12). How might one locate and characterise this so-called 'natural "organic" unity'? For Curl this is the central distinguishing feature of the field of Human Movement Studies, but in what sense might its subject matter have a 'natural unity'? Certainly the whole area contains its own distinctive focus, and its supporting conceptual systems relate to each other in a way that provides a degree of internal coherence. But to describe this coherence as 'organic', even if the term is being used metaphorically, is misleading. The mind and body might relate to each other organically during different movement activities, but it does not necessarily follow that this state of affairs can be built into the characterisation of the field of study.

Academic study of Human Movement at tertiary education level

Human Movement can be studied for both intrinsic and extrinsic reasons; that is, either as an activity pursued for its own sake or as an area of professional concern in which the ends are largely instrumental in kind. At the level of tertiary education such study can take three forms: the academic study of the different kinds of theoretical and practical knowledge that contribute to Human Movement; actual engagement in different forms of human movement; and the applied study of Human Movement, as in the case of teacher education. The academic study would comprise the disinterested, objective pursuit of philosophy and the physical and human sciences with the intention of providing a wide range of theoretical insights into the heterogeneous forms of human movement. With its emphasis on developing a clear perception and cognitive grasp of the contributory modes of thought, academic study would enable a person to reflect critically and imaginatively on the nature of each discipline, to master the different methods of inquiry, and to draw out the wide-ranging conceptual interconnections between each form of understanding. Serious engagement in this form of study would sensitise a student to the distinctions, similarities and relationships between different structures of thought, but it would focus also on the conceptual coherence of the whole field of knowledge. As its primary concern is the development of certain qualities of mind, powers of reasoning and the capacity for general ideas, such academic study would bring a student to the point of raising fundamental questions as to the value, assumptions, standards and scope of the disciplines contributing to Human

Movement Studies. Thus it would enable him to build up a personal commitment to and a concern for the activity.

Several elements would constitute the basis of this academic study. Initially, philosophical analysis could demonstrate that human movement itself is not a uniform global phenomenon and that there is no one mode of experience which could be regarded as 'movement knowledge' or 'movement understanding' (Redfern 1973, pp. 133–4). For instance, an important distinction has to be drawn between those mindless physical movements that just happen to us, such as nervous twitches and reflex movements, and those consciously conceived actions which presuppose the rational formulation of intentions within a particular frame of reference. Many physical actions contain habitual and routinisable elements, but nevertheless they remain preformed motor skills which are related to the perception of the world, and as such are logically very different in kind from involuntary sensory, protection and defence reflexes. Moreover, in the area of consciously determined physical action, further distinctions need to be made between the many different forms of human movement in the light of the purpose, function and context of each action. As Betty Redfern (1973) indicates, movement experience should become 'increasingly diversified as different ways of directing and organising it are developed according to the particular purposes which it may serve' (p. 139). Such diverse kinds of movement as dance, mime, conversational gesture, gross operational movements, athletic movements and ritualistic movements can hardly be viewed as a homogeneous unity. In each case the form of movement experience must contain its own unique features, its own mode of operation, its own standards of appraisal and its own criteria of appropriateness. Philosophy then, more especially philosophical psychology, enables us to differentiate out and to characterise the many forms and functions of human movement in the light of the intentions and aims of the agent. Areas that might be examined in a course of study could include:

(a) the development of mind;

(b) the relationship between mind and body;
(c) the relationship between thought and action;
(d) causes, motives, intentions and action;
(e) the distinction between bodily movement and physical action;
(f) different kinds of movement understanding.

Some movement forms, for example dance and mime, and to a lesser extent activities like gymnastics, diving, skating and trampolining, contain certain distinctive features which can be analysed and appraised through another branch of philosophy—namely, aesthetics. It has been suggested (Layson, 1973, pp. 111–19) that the aesthetic dimension of movement can be viewed in two ways: through an examination of the possible aesthetic qualities internal to the activity itself; or by considering both the aesthetic experience of the individual performer and the aesthetic attitude of the spectator. By focusing on the nature of different physical activities it is possible to place each on a continuum or spectrum according to the way in which they display such aesthetic properties as form, style, balance, harmony, grace, symmetry, rhythm, line and economy of effort (Anthony, 1968, pp. 2–3; Reid, 1970, pp. 6–7). At one end of the continuum would lie those kinds of dance which satisfy the conditions of an art form. Although there are dances such as fertility dances, war-dances and pop dancing whose ends are largely instrumental in character, these need to be contrasted with those dances whose structured movements become objects of disinterested, aesthetic contemplation (Redfern, 1973, pp. 139–41; Reid, 1970, p. 21). In such cases the aesthetic properties are essential to the dance. Logically they are constitutive of the activity, and attempting to grasp the meanings embodied in these formal features becomes one of the main aims of either engaging in or watching the dance. The fundamental purpose of the movement in dance, then, is aesthetic. At the other end of this continuum lie those physical activities, such as games and sports, the central point of which is winning, scoring points or the achievement of technical efficiency. A games-player might gain some aes-

thetic satisfaction from the contemplation of his performance retrospectively, perhaps through a visual recording.
Equally, a spectator might adopt an aesthetic attitude towards a game or sport. But in these cases the aesthetic element
is incidental to the main aim of the activity (Reid, 1969a, pp.
7–8). As Reid (1970) indicates, 'the aesthetic enjoyment is
parasitic upon the central games-purpose of the game' (p.
17). In between these two extremes of the continuum lie
those activities like gymnastics, diving, skating and trampolining in which one of the aims might be considered
aesthetic. In many instances competition would remain the
major objective, but as certain artistic elements would also
be of central concern, any appraisal would have to refer in
part to particular aesthetic criteria (Reid, 1970, pp. 18–20).

It can be seen from these different examples that if we are
to make appropriate judgments about art and the aesthetic in
relation to movement, it is necessary for the student of
Human Movement to examine certain aspects of aesthetics.
Such a course of study could include:

(a) the distinction between 'work of art' and 'aesthetic
    object';
(b) the elements of a work of art;
(c) knowledge and understanding in the arts;
(d) aesthetic experience as a way of knowing;
(e) the nature of aesthetic meaning;
(f) movement and meaning;
(g) dance as an art form;
(h) aesthetic appraisal in relation to different forms of
    human movement.

Although this dual philosophical perspective of aesthetics
and philosophical psychology can contribute to our thinking
about the nature of human movement, a fuller understanding
can be acquired only through those empirical descriptions
and explanations culled from the physical and human
sciences. This dimension has been fairly comprehensively
explored in recent years (especially Brooke and Whiting,
1973) and areas that might be studied include:

(a) physical aspects of human development;
(b) different methods of movement analysis;
(c) factors affecting the acquisition of perceptual-motor skills;
(d) psychological study of skilled behaviour;
(e) personality and movement behaviour;
(f) patterns of human movement within society;
(g) the place of movement in inter-personal communication and social interaction;
(h) the role of dance, games and sport within different socio-cultural contexts;
(i) the history of dance, games and sport.

Engagement in different forms of human movement

So far the discussion has been limited to those aspects of Human Movement Studies that might be considered appropriate for academic, theoretical study at the level of tertiary education. This should have demonstrated that Human Movement can be pursued for intrinsic reasons and that it can be viewed successfully outside the more limited confines of a professional context. Nevertheless, the understanding gained from this academic study would be strengthened considerably if students were to engage also in a range of physical activities designed to illustrate different forms of movement experience; these might include, for example, dance, gymnastics, athletics and games. Such an approach should meet the objection (North, 1971, p. 11) that courses in Movement Studies might focus unduly on propositional or theoretical knowledge (i.e. 'knowing about' facts, rules and principles) to the possible exclusion of practical knowledge (i.e. 'knowing how to' perform a skill), thus depriving the activity of its prime *raison d'être*. A balanced programme would need to stress the dual importance of the participant and spectator roles (Adams, 1969, pp. 32–4; Layson, 1970, p. 250), thereby establishing a close relationship between the different areas of academic study and the actual pursuit of movement itself.

For example, in the study of dance, apart from acquiring the technical knowledge necessary for engaging in the activity, it is essential to learn how to examine the nature of dance, how to view the purpose of dance in a variety of contexts, how to appreciate dance as an observer, how to 'watch' or 'visualise' oneself dancing and how to critically appraise the aesthetic quality of a dance. All these abilities presuppose a cognitive grasp of public rules and standards, which can be located and developed only through different kinds of propositional and practical knowledge. Sometimes the importance of this public dimension is underplayed. For instance, in her emphasis on the relationship between the 'inner being' of the person moving and the 'outer form' of the movement itself, Marion North (1968) sees the study of Movement leading towards 'the formulating of inner experiences' (p. 9). Apart from the vagueness of this kind of language, her account neglects the public nature of the conscious, intentional activity of dance. Achievements in dance, along with those in other physical activities, are not basically 'inner' and private, as is suggested by Peter Arnold (1973, p. 21). The meanings embodied in all deliberately planned movements are conceived and expressed in public symbols. They might have personal significance for the individual performer or spectator, but essentially they are public in nature and need to be submitted to some form of independent check in accordance with the criteria considered appropriate for that particular context.

An understanding of dance, then, will be facilitated by knowledge gained from the disciplines contributing to Human Movement Studies. On the other hand, unlike the many physical activities which are not art forms, the study of dance would be emasculated if it focused solely on different kinds of propositional and practical knowledge to the exclusion of 'acquaintance-knowledge', which is fundamental to aesthetic experience (Reid, 1973, p. 68). 'Knowing' movement through the medium of dance must involve the experiential side of coming to know which can be achieved only through direct engagement or confrontation between the person and the dance form itself (Greger, 1972). The

relationship established between the two takes on the character of friendship (Elliott, 1972, p. 122), and it helps to foster
a strong sense of knowing which not only constitutes the
core of an aesthetic experience but also cannot be reduced to
either 'knowing how' or 'knowing that'. Of course, this is a
highly controversial area of philosophy, and those protagonists committed to an over-propositional view of knowledge
would deny the claims to knowledge in the various non-
discursive forms of understanding. For instance, the analytic
propositions of mathematics, which contain logically necessary truths, would satisfy the conditions of knowledge. The
synthetic or empirical statements of science, where truth
rests on contingent fact and strong probability, might possibly be considered another form of knowledge. But many
philosophers would characterise the 'enriched acquaintance'
embodied in aesthetic knowledge as a mode of experience
rather than a form of knowing. They might accept that
aesthetic experience is a mode of cognition, but they would
deny that any response displaying the features of unanalys-
able, unverifiable 'intuition' could count as knowledge. It
would seem that this is a very restricted view of what
constitutes knowledge, and that perhaps the term should be
used in an extended sense to include 'the process of coming
to know', which cannot be expressed in propositions. As
Reid (1969b) indicates, 'the only adequate language of the
elucidation of art is the language of art itself' (p. 219), and I
would wish to support his contention that acquaintance-
knowledge is a way of knowing which is a salient feature of
all the performing arts (1969b, p. 214). This means that of
all the areas that one might be studying through the disciplines of Human Movement, an education in dance particularly would comprise an initiation into several distinctive conceptual structures based on different kinds of
propositional and practical knowledge, together with an aesthetic insight gained from acquaintance-knowledge.

The study of Human Movement within the context of teacher education

The study of Human Movement, then, can take the form of disinterested academic inquiry, supported by the pursuit of different kinds of movement experience. But as was stated earlier, it can be studied also within an applied frame of reference for instrumental reasons. For example, in teacher education a student could engage in the academic study of Human Movement, partnered by the necessary practical and acquaintance-knowledge, but pursued within a broad professional context (Renshaw, 1973a, pp. 227–35). This form of study could well be conducted within the unit-based curricular framework suggested by the government White Paper, *Education: A Framework for Expansion* (1972, pars. 75–8). This would enable students to pursue a two-year Diploma of Higher Education, designed within a teacher education context and leading on to either a three-year Ordinary B.Ed. degree or a four-year Honours B.Ed. degree.

A student could take Human Movement Studies as his core (or main) subject, supported by two or three related contextual or cognate subjects such as music and drama. The professional dimension of each subject area could comprise four inter-related elements:

(a) the value and place of the subject in education, including the aims underlying the teaching of the subject and the justification for including it on the school curriculum;
(b) the psychological aspects of learning the subject;
(c) the sociological dimension of teaching the subject;
(d) appropriate learning experiences and teaching methods in schools.

In order to attain a measure of structural coherence within the curriculum, these four elements would have to be planned and studied in conjunction with certain parts of the Education course. For example, units in philosophy, psychology and sociology of education might include the following topics which could be considered significant for the teacher of Human Movement.

Unit in philosophy of education

(a) The contribution of philosophy to curriculum planning.
(b) Procedural principles, curriculum aims and objectives.
(c) Curriculum justifications.
(d) Education and the development of mind.
(e) Learning and teaching.
(f) Play and learning by discovery.
(g) Thinking and concept formation.
(h) Propositional, practical and acquaintance-knowledge.
(i) Analytic, empirical and normative statements.
(j) The structure of knowledge; different ways of knowing.
(k) Discursive and non-discursive forms of understanding.
(l) Curriculum integration.

Unit in educational psychology

(a) Stages of human development.
(b) Children's levels of thinking.
(c) Concept acquisition.
(d) Learning and motivation.
(e) The place of language in learning experiences.
(f) Evaluation procedures and testing.
(g) The bases of social behaviour.
(h) Interpersonal behaviour.

Unit in sociology of education

(a) Socio-cultural processes which affect human development and behaviour.

(b) The school and the classroom as social systems.
(c) The role of the teacher.
(d) Socio-linguistic factors in learning.
(e) The 'hidden' curriculum.
(f) The social organisation of knowledge.
(g) The distribution of knowledge in schools and the implications for multi-disciplinary areas of study.
(h) Problems of power, order and control arising from different types of curricula.

The ultimate aim of the whole course of study would be the development of a theoretical frame of reference which would not only enable a student to engage in different movement activities with an informed understanding, but would also illuminate the practical and social skills involved in the teaching of Human Movement. It would be hoped that a professional education of this nature would raise the academic and professional standards of the teacher of Human Movement, and thus contribute to the creation of a knowledge-based profession. The teacher's professional authority and autonomy can hardly rest on an unreflective pragmatism which spurns rational self-evaluation. His judgments need to be supported by a systematic body of theory in which principles are formulated through empirical research and logical analysis, and then related to the realities of teaching. It is questionable, though, whether such a body of knowledge can be located which could claim to constitute 'physical education theory', as has been suggested by Curl (1973, p. 13). It would seem more logical to view the study of physical education in colleges in terms of the development of an understanding of principles, concepts, skills and methods of inquiry drawn from Human Movement, and related in turn to the study of children and to the educational process. It is not meaningful to talk about 'biological education theory' or 'historical education theory'; therefore it is difficult to see why physical education can claim legitimately to have its own unique body of theoretical knowledge. This view is supported by Abernathy and Waltz (1964) who state that 'the justification (of physical education) in the long run, will rest upon the utilisation of principles drawn from scholarly inquiry into the phenomenon of human movement' (p. 6). They regard physical education as knowledge of Human Movement applied within an educational context (also Siedentop, 1972, pp. 95–6).

The study of Human Movement in schools

At present it is comparatively rare to find fully developed courses in Human Movement Studies in schools. The majority of first and middle schools tend to focus, quite appropriately, on a wide range of physical activities designed primarily to promote an enjoyment and satisfaction in the vigorous movements of the body. As children reach the middle years of schooling (i.e. 8–13 years of age) greater emphasis is placed on the disciplined acquisition of physical skills, while dance and mime are likely to assume a central place in aesthetic education programmes. But at the level of secondary education there is a growing interest in developing the theoretical as well as the practical study of Human Movement (Arnold, 1973, p. 19; Layson, 1969, p. 53; Mauldon, 1970, p. 18). For instance, Nuffield Secondary Science (1971) has taken 'Movement' as one of its themes, and it has devoted a whole section to an examination of 'The Natural Movement of Living Things' (pp. 103–59). This particular unit of study is keen to make explicit the distinction between the random movements of the biologically lower orders and the conscious, purposive physical actions of thinking and reasoning human beings. One of its main aims is to encourage pupils to find out

> . . . something of the extent to which purpose, as a conscious determination, enters into daily life, and the extent to which their own movements are also governed by random factors and sub-conscious purposes very like those of the lower creatures (p. 109).

Several of the individual topics in the Nuffield scheme could well be incorporated into a Human Movement Studies programme: e.g.

(a) movement for a purpose;
(b) balance (including the scientific principles underlying an understanding of movement in athletics);
(c) momentum (including rotation);
(d) walking, running and jumping;
(e) projectiles;
(f) flight;
(g) swimming.

Although many of the schools that have developed theoretical courses in Human Movement have tended to concentrate on those explanations and descriptions which draw on the physical sciences, there are fruitful channels to be explored in other directions. For example, some older secondary pupils might find the study of the ecology of movement behaviour valuable and interesting. The aim of such a course would be to examine the ways in which man moves and interacts with both the natural and social environment (Jewett and Mullan, 1972, p. 83). Topics could include:

(a) physical aspects of human development;
(b) patterns of human movement within society;
(c) attitudes towards physical activity;
(d) the contribution of movement activities to social interaction;
(e) non-verbal communication;
(f) the role of dance, games and sport within different societies.

Within this course, an inquiry into different cultural influences on movement participation could be based on the societal classification outlined by Hendry (1973, pp. 143–52). This movement classification contains several interrelated areas of study: e.g.

(a) goal-directed movements;
(b) excitatory movements;
(c) bizarre movements;
(d) aesthetic movements;
(e) communicative movement;
(f) group status and its effect on human movement;

(g) ritualistic movement;

(h) protest movement;

(i) stillness and the containment of movement.

Finally, Human Movement could contribute to a multi-disciplinary programme designed to focus on certain key concepts. For instance, the grasp of an aesthetic concept like 'form', 'structure', 'symmetry', 'balance' or 'line' can be approached through the study of mathematics, dance, music, drama, poetry, painting and sculpture. The starting point for such a project could arise from within any of these activities (e.g. a Bridget Riley painting, an electronic composition by Stockhausen or a mathematical structure), but the primary aim would be to examine the meaning and use of particular aesthetic concepts in a number of different contexts. Another example of a multi-disciplinary approach could arise from a study of the different ways in which the concepts 'function' and 'form' relate to each other. Again, a variety of contexts could be taken ranging from games, swimming and gymnastics to such disparate activities as playing the violin, constructing a bridge, designing an aeroplane and making a kinetic art object.

This section has offered some tentative suggestions for the theoretical study of Human Movement in schools, especially at the level of secondary education. Nevertheless, the proviso ought to be made, as it was earlier in the chapter, that the acquisition of propositional knowledge about human movement remains a limited kind of education if it is not supported by the actual pursuit of different forms of movement experience.

The educational value of Human Movement Studies and Physical Education

At the heart of educational debate lie problems arising from the justification of different types of curricular activities. Thus it is necessary to examine how far Human Movement Studies and physical education might be placed on the curriculum for educational reasons, or whether the grounds which support their inclusion are more instrumental in character. Ruth Morison (1969) has asserted that 'the inclusion of physical education as part of the school curriculum needs no justification' (p. 2), but a commitment to a rational notion of morality, with its implicit respect for persons and concern for truth, demands that teachers justify all the activities in a curriculum. The value of physical education can hardly masquerade as a self-evident truth, as is recognised by Jelfs (1970) when he suggests that 'to assume that physical education is an area of educational activity is an assumption of immense proportions—it is no longer any use saying that we all know this is true' (pp. 117–18). The fundamental question then, is how far do Human Movement Studies and physical education measure up to the criteria built into the concept 'education'?

The descriptive and the evaluative definitions of education

In order to answer this question a distinction between two different types of language usage needs to be made explicit, because the concept 'education' can function in both a descriptive and an evaluative sense. A descriptive definition is intended to explain the meaning of a term by giving an account of its prior, common usage. It tries to clarify the normal everyday use of a word, and although some descriptive statements contain an implicit programme of action, logically such prescriptions cannot be derived from descriptions (see Scheffler, 1960, Chapter 1). Therefore, education might be described quite legitimately as a form of national investment; different educational systems can be described and contrasted; a teacher might describe his career in education. Similarly, the term physical education can be used purely descriptively to embrace all the physical activities that go on in schools. In each case the word education is being used to describe a certain state of affairs which carries no normative implications; each statement is value-neutral.

On the other hand, the evaluative use implies that those engaged in education value it for intrinsic reasons (Wilson,

1971, p. 121), and that they pursue it purposefully to develop certain intrinsically desirable qualities of mind based on a breadth and depth of knowledge and understanding (Hirst and Peters, 1970, p. 25). One of the central values implicit in this evaluative concept is that of rational autonomy (see Dearden, 1972; Downie and Telfer, 1971). It is assumed that education is concerned with the development of the critically reflective person—one who is not a pale reflection of a situation defined and conceived of by some significant other, but who can adopt a rationally critical stance towards himself and society. Such an education enables a person to stand back and reflect on the central features of the dialectic taking place between himself and the social world, and it gives him the opportunity to choose his own distinctive frame of reference and value-position from the many contradictory norms and values to which he is exposed. It sharpens his selective antennae, thus allowing him to pursue consciously formulated ends and to choose for himself between alternative courses of action. The choices and decisions made by an autonomous person are authentic in so far as they are made in the light of the individual's own rationally determined moral position, rather than being controlled by external events. They bear the hallmark of an assertive point of view, which submits all socially prescribed roles and rules to critical scrutiny. Education, on this view, is focused essentially on the search for truth and on the development of a personal autonomy exercised within a framework of moral responsibility (Renshaw, 1973b).

It must be apparent that this evaluative sense of education does not profess to reflect prior common usage. The meaning of the term education in this context contains a stipulation as well as implying a programme of action that requires further justification. This raises fundamental philosophical dilemmas which are rarely resolved. But suffice it to say that the value-judgments and prescriptions implicit in the concept 'education' can be justified only in terms of a particular ethical view of what constitutes a 'person', the grounds of which can be supported by a transcendental process of reasoning which suggests that an evaluative, moral concept of 'person' is the necessary presupposition of morality. Central to this concept of 'person' is the notion of autonomy, and if we value persons we must necessarily respect their autonomy to exactly the same degree that we value our own. It follows that if one is committed to this ethical position, education must be seen essentially as a concern for the development of a personal autonomy based on reason.

In the light of this argument we can pose the question again as to how far Human Movement Studies and physical education measure up to the criteria built into this evaluative concept of education. From our earlier discussion of the different ways of knowing that contribute to an understanding of Human Movement, it would appear that not only can the whole area of study be pursued for its own sake, but that the nature of the knowledge gained can make a significant contribution to the development of mind, which is so central to the process of becoming an autonomous person. Thus, as an activity Human Movement Studies satisfies both the value and cognitive conditions of the concept 'education' (see Hirst and Peters, 1970, pp. 85–6). This claim can also be substantiated for the study of dance which, although viewed sometimes as a means to an extrinsic end (e.g. personal satisfaction, emotional experience, moral awareness, social cohesion or interpersonal understanding—Redfern, 1973, p. 141), really needs no further justification beyond itself when conceived as an aesthetic experience. But how far can the same case be made for the narrower applied field of Physical Education? Certainly such wide-ranging activities as games, gymnastics, swimming, athletics, orienteering and leisure pursuits can be partially illuminated by the study of Human Movement, but how far can they be considered of educational value in the evaluative sense of the term (Carlisle, 1969, pp. 13–16; Renshaw, 1972a, pp. 63–4)?

In order to answer this question it is necessary to examine the intention of the person engaged in the relevant activity. How does the teacher or the student view the point of the activity? Are his objectives instrumental or intrinsic in kind? Games, for example, might be characterised as self-contained physical pursuits involving skills of a specific nature with a limited cognitive content. They can be pursued for extrinsic reasons, but they can also be engaged in for the competition internal to many games and for the satisfaction derived from the physical movement itself. Although the object of games is hardly the disinterested pursuit of truth (which is one of the central characteristics of a theoretical activity), both Carlisle (1969, p. 16) and Wilson (1971, p. 89) are right to distinguish between 'playing a game properly' and 'playing about'. If a game is entertained seriously and is pursued in a disciplined way, thus displaying a knowledge of public rules and standards, we can say that the activity is educational in the task sense of the word. Although games might not satisfy the wider cognitive conditions of education, it is possible to engage in them seriously for intrinsic reasons. Games, then, can be viewed as part of the educational process if a student is encouraged to structure his movements and consciousness according to the public standards internal to the activity. The emphasis must be on knowledge with understanding, thus allowing for critical objective appraisal, rather than on mindless physical drill and conditioning (also Peters, 1967, pp. 9–10).

But how far are physical activities pursued in schools and colleges for such educational reasons? Recent literature throws up certain objectives in physical education which would be characterised more appropriately as instrumental in kind. For example, how far can such aims as the promotion of physical fitness and health, the acquisition of neuromuscular skills, the development of social adjustment, the development of emotional stability and the formation of a positive attitude towards physical activity be considered *educational* (Andrews, 1970; Hendry, 1970; Rosentswieg, 1969; Wilson, 1969)? As such objectives might serve a useful purpose external to the activity itself, it would seem more logical to view them as the ends of some therapeutic or socialisation process. But they can hardly masquerade as valid aims of physical *education*, if the term 'education' is functioning in an evaluative rather than a descriptive sense. When Williams (1970) argues, for instance, that 'the whole idea of functional physical education is to transform the initial locomotor . . ., manipulative movements and the urge to play with and acquire skilled movement, into tools, and thus lead to full functional and recreative efficiency' (pp. 58–9), he seems to be making an effective case for physical *training* rather than education. This is not to imply that objectives like the promotion of fitness, health, functional and recreative efficiency are not valid in themselves, but that they display the features of an instrumental rather than an educational end.

Finally, how do games measure up to the achievement aspects of education? It has been maintained that a wide cognitive frame of reference can be gained through the systematic study of Human Movement, but can such physical activities as games and sports develop a similar breadth of understanding and discernment? On the one hand, it might be possible to demonstrate that education can be achieved through the medium of games. In such a case the physical activity is no longer regarded merely as a game, but rather as a means for developing such qualities of mind as aesthetic awareness, moral judgment and inter-personal understanding (Peters, 1966, p. 159). On the other hand, when a game is pursued purely as a game, it fails to satisfy the wider cognitive conditions of education. This is not to suggest that games do not have any cognitive content. Many games require considerable knowledge, understanding and discrimination. This is particularly so in the case of complex 'open' skills (like golf and football), which demand a high degree of perceptual judgment, as distinct from the more habitual 'closed' skills (like shot-putting and diving) at the other end of the continuum (see Knapp, 1961; Knapp, 1964; Whiting, 1969). Nevertheless, all skills, whether they be 'open' or 'closed', are essentially specific in nature. They contain their own internal cognitive content but their scope is limited. Although a distinction might be drawn between general strategic dispositional skills and those techniques with a limited range of application, all skills nevertheless operate only within a specific context. Rules might be extended and the conception of a game might change over the course of time, but skills cannot generate new meanings as can the art form of dance and neither can they illuminate other activities. It is this specific character of skills which leads us to talk about *training* in games or sports rather than education.

Many of the issues raised in this chapter are germane to the current inquiry into the nature and status of physical education and into its relationship with Human Movement Studies. Philosophy by itself cannot possibly solve these complex problems, but it can help to refine and to reformulate the questions that need to be asked. This type of critical reappraisal might give the teacher a new perspective with which to view his task, and in time this might lead to radical changes in both the structure and study of physical education and Human Movement in schools and colleges.

References

ABERNATHY, R. and WALTZ, M. (1964) 'Toward a discipline: first steps first'. *Quest*, **II**, 1–7.

ADAMS, M. (1969) 'The concept of physical education'. *Proceedings of the Annual Conference, Philosophy of Education Society of Great Britain*, **III**, 23–35.

ANDREWS, J. C. (1970) 'Physical education and education'. *Bulletin of Physical Education*, **VIII** (3), 21–7.

ANTHONY, D. W. J. (1968) 'Sport and physical education as a means of aesthetic education'. *Bulletin of Physical Education*, **60** (179), 1–6.

ARNOLD, P. J. (1973) 'Education and the concept of movement'. *Bulletin of Physical Education*, **IX** (5), 13–22.

BROOKE, J. D. and WHITING, H. T. A. (eds) (1973) *Human Movement—a field of study*. Kimpton: London.

CARLISLE, R. (1969) 'The concept of physical education'. *Proceedings of the Annual Conference, Philosophy of Education Society of Great Britain*, **III**, 5–22.

CURL, G. F. (1973) 'An attempt to justify Human Movement as a field of study' in BROOKE, J. D. and WHITING, H. T. A. (eds) *Human Movement—a field of study*. Kimpton: London.

DEARDEN, R. F. (1972) 'Autonomy and education' in DEARDEN, R. F., HIRST, P. H. and PETERS, R. S. (eds) *Education and the Development of Reason*. Routledge and Kegan Paul: London.

DOWNIE, R. S. and TELFER, E. (1971) 'Autonomy'. *Philosophy* **XLVI** (178), 293–301.

Education: A Framework for Expansion (1972) Cmnd 5174. HMSO: London.

ELLIOTT, R. K. (1972) 'The critic and the lover of art' in MAYS, W. and BROWN, S. C. (eds) *Linguistic Analysis and Phenomenology.* Macmillan: London.

GREGER, S. (1972) 'Aesthetic meaning'. *Proceedings of the Philosophy of Education Society of Great Britain,* **VI** (2), 137–63.

HENDRY, A. E. (1970) 'The expansion of the curriculum and physical education'. *British Journal of Physical Education,* **1** (5), 101–103.

HENDRY, L. B. (1973) 'Human movement: a societal study' in BROOKE, J. D. and WHITING, H. T. A. (eds) *Human Movement—a field of study.* Kimpton: London.

HINKS, E. M., ARCHBUTT, S. E. and CURL, G. F. (1971) 'Movement studies: a new standing committee'. *University of London Institute of Education Bulletin,* **23,** 4–10.

HIRST, P. H. and PETERS, R. S. (1970) *The Logic of Education.* Routledge and Kegan Paul: London.

JELFS, B. W. (1970) 'Thinking about the meaning of physical education'. *British Journal of Physical Education,* **1,** 117–18.

JEWETT, A. E. and MULLAN, M. R. (1972) 'A conceptual model for teacher education'. *Quest,* **XVIII,** 76–87.

KNAPP, B. N. (1961) 'A note on skill'. *Occupational Psychology,* **35,** 76–8.

KNAPP, B. N. (1964) *Skill in Sport.* Routledge and Kegan Paul: London.

LAYSON, J. E. (1969) 'An introduction to some aspects of the sociology of physical education' in Conference report on *Physical Education: Aesthetic and Social Aspects.* Association of Principals of Women's Colleges of Physical Education.

LAYSON, J. E. (1970) 'The contribution of modern dance to education'. Unpublished MEd thesis, Manchester University.

LAYSON, J. E. (1973) 'Aesthetics and human movement' in BROOKE, J. D. and WHITING, H. T. A. (eds) *Human Movement—a field of study.* Kimpton: London.

MAULDON, B. (1970) 'What is physical education?' *Bulletin of Physical Education,* **VIII** (3), 13–20.

MAWDSLEY, H. P. (1971) 'A conceptual analysis of human movement'. *Bulletin of Physical Education,* **VIII** (5), 39–45.

MORISON, R. (1969) *A Movement Approach to Educational Gymnastics.* Dent: London.

NORTH, M. (1968) 'Movement—a new academic field?' *University of London Institute of Education Bulletin,* **15,** 7–13.

NORTH, M. (1971) 'But where is the movement? A critique'. *University of London Institute of Education Bulletin,* **23,** 11–12.

Nuffield Secondary Science (1971) Theme 6. *Movement.* Longman: London.

PETERS, R. S. (1966) *Ethics and Education.* Allen and Unwin: London.

PETERS, R. S. (ed.) (1967) *The Concept of Education.* Routledge and Kegan Paul: London.

REDFERN, H. B. (1973) *Concepts in Modern Educational Dance.* Kimpton: London.

REID, L. A. (1969a) 'Aesthetics and education'. Conference report on *Physical Education: Aesthetic and Social Aspects.* Association of Principals of Women's Colleges of Physical Education.

REID, L. A. (1969b) *Meaning in the Arts.* Allen and Unwin: London.

REID, L. A. (1970) 'Movement and meaning'. *Laban Art of Movement Guild Magazine,* **45,** 5–31.

REID, L. A. (1973) 'Knowledge, aesthetic insight and education'. *Proceedings of the Philosophy of Education Society of Great Britain,* **VII** (1), 66–84.

RENSHAW, P. (1972a) 'Physical education: the need for philosophical clarification'. *Education for Teaching,* **87,** 60–68.

RENSHAW, P. (1972b) 'The nature of human movement studies and its relationship with physical education'. *Cambridge Journal of Education,* **2** (2), 92–106.

RENSHAW, P. (1973a) 'A flexible curriculum for teacher education' in LOMAX, D. E. (ed.) *The Education of Teachers in Britain.* Wiley: London.

RENSHAW, P. (1973b) 'Socialisation: the negation of education?' *Journal of Moral Education,* **2** (3), 211–20.

ROSENTSWIEG, J. (1969) 'A ranking of the objectives of physical education'. *Research Quarterly,* **40** (4), 783–87.

SCHEFFLER, I. (1960) *The Language of Education.* Thomas: Springfield, Illinois.

SIEDENTOP, D. (1972) 'On tilting at windmills while Rome burns'. *Quest,* **XVIII,** 94–7.

WEBB, I. M. (1970) 'Nomenclature, taxonomy or what's in a name?' *British Journal of Physical Education,* **I** (1), 3–5.

WHITING, H. T. A. (1969) *Acquiring Ball Skill.* G. Bell: London.

WILLIAMS, L. C. (1970) 'Art and Science of movement'. *British Journal of Physical Education,* **1** (3), 58–63.

WILSON, C. (1969) 'Diversities in meanings of physical education'. *Research Quarterly,* **40** (1), 211–14.

WILSON, P. S. (1971) *Interest and Discipline in Education.* Routledge and Kegan Paul: London.

CHAPTER THREE

The Schools Council Inquiry—Interpretation and Social Context

John E. Kane

The Schools Council for Curriculum and Examination was set up in 1964 for the purpose of reviewing and reforming the curriculum in England and Wales. Since then the pace with which the curriculum research and development movement has grown has surprised even its most ardent supporters. In the year immediately before the establishment of the Schools Council the main research agency in this field, the NFER, had an income of £41,000, whereas grants from the Department of Education and the local education authorities to the Schools Council had risen to £1,674,000 by 1973. The recent attitude towards curriculum research and development may be gauged by indicating the amount of financial support allocated to a few of the many recent Schools Council projects: Modern Languages Project—£894,000; Project Technology—£287,000; Humanities Curriculum Project—£174,000.

The challenge of the curriculum reform movement has come relatively late to physical education. The forces that have reshaped, for example, the science, mathematics and language curricula, have only just begun to affect physical education. This in itself may be more of a help than a hindrance if the pitfalls of the early curriculum 'mongering' and the over-enthusiasm of curriculum innovators can be avoided. It seems likely, however, that there will be increasing pressure on teachers of physical education to make explicit their curriculum purposes and the principles by which they plan for and judge effective achievement. These are matters that all teachers have to consider constantly and that most teachers find difficult. Taylor (1970), for instance, in a recent assessment considers that while teachers in general are probably aware of the complexities underlying the process of curriculum planning, they do not appear to have developed a satisfactory procedure for systematically taking them into account. As a first stage towards helping physical education teachers to review and reform the secondary schools curriculum the Schools Council sponsored an Inquiry to discover details of current practices in physical education and the relationship of these practices to the aims of the subject and, in general, to provide up-to-date evidence on which curriculum development projects might be based. The Inquiry has recently been published (Kane, 1974) and represents a survey of concepts, practices and experiences which are central to current programmes in physical education. The evidence was largely collected from teachers in a one-in-ten sample of secondary schools in England and Wales. Much of what follows in this chapter is an elaboration and speculation of some major curriculum issues deriving from the information supplied in the Inquiry. Before proceeding to such detailed discussion it may be useful to consider the broader context, and, particularly, the social context in which curriculum research and development is currently taking place.

Some social factors in curriculum development

As Hoyle (1971) points out, we know too little at present about the process of educational innovation in general and curriculum renewal in particular. He does attempt, however, to summarise some of the main elements within and outside the school which are involved in a consideration of curriculum change and the diffusion of innovation (Figure 3.1).

The prevailing social system represented in Box 1 is taken to be directly reflected in our educational structure (Box 2) and distally affects the process of curricular change through value systems centred on, for example, class structure, econ-

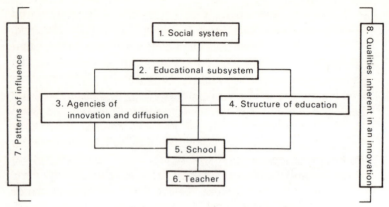

Figure 3.1   Influences on curriculum change (Hoyle 1971)

omic pressures and the social determinants of educability. Social and educational change are assumed to be related though the complex nature of the relationship is not well understood. Box 3 takes into account the agencies of innovation which include, for example, the Schools Council, and other research units, teacher-training institutions, Her Majesty's Inspectorate and professional organisations. Box 4 represents the structure of education and the relative effect on curriculum change of the local, national and private contributions. Boxes 5 and 6 show the position of the school and the teacher in the reciprocal flow of influences. Hoyle adds two additional groups of variables that have pervasive effects on the curriculum process. These are referred to as 'patterns of influence' (Box 7), which focus attention on forms of authority and inter-personal influences, and 'qualities inherent in an innovation' (Box 8) which affect the rate and extent of its acceptance to an adopting system.

Apart from these general factors, which are suggested to account for the major extrinsic influences affecting curriculum change, some investigators have considered the relationship between the internal school climate (Box 5) and the effectiveness of innovatory approaches. It would appear that for genuine innovation to 'take' in a school, the teachers concerned must be highly committed to ensuring its success and it may be that there are certain personal characteristics predisposing some teachers to experiment and adopt changes. Of greater importance, however, is what has been referred to as the 'organisational health' of the school (Miles 1964). A school in good organisational health might be expected to demonstrate a willingness for continuing self-analysis, to be susceptible to opportunities for innovation and effectively to assimilate appropriate innovations. One of the few studies on the characteristics of schools likely to be receptive to curriculum innovation has been undertaken by Halpin (1967) who described six distinct 'organisation climates' which range from 'open' to 'closed'. In summary the six climates which relate to the behaviour of the staff and the school principal are suggested as:

(a) *'open'*—describing the positive but flexible leadership of the principal;
(b) *'autonomous'*—describing a climate in which the principal gives less positive leadership but more autonomy to teachers;
(c) *'controlled'*—where the principal is more authoritarian and controls his staff closely but where the staff derive satisfaction (as they do in 'open' and 'autonomous' climates) in their task achievements;
(d) *'familiar'*—where the principal is concerned with providing a happy family atmosphere rather than leadership but where the staff have little task satisfaction;
(e) *'paternal'*—characterised by over-solicitous behaviour of the principal linked with poor control and giving rise to poor staff motivation;
(f) *'closed'*—describing an aloof, disregarding and impersonal stance by the principal which gives rise to little or no task or social satisfactions among the staff.

Such organisational climates differentially affect both the kind of investment which the teacher may make in the educational process and also the satisfaction which he derives from it (Box 6). As a result of his perception of the prevailing climate and his personalised reaction to it, the teacher presumably devises and adopts an acceptable role, which may be described, according to Corwin (1965), on a continuum extending from an employee model to a professional model. The employee teacher is described as one who works strictly within the institutionalised rules, uses standardised techniques in teaching and has a low susceptibility to innovation. In contrast, the professional teacher is characterised by Corwin as flexible, problem-oriented and innovative. Clearly curriculum change and renewal are more likely to occur in schools typifying an 'open' organisational climate and in which teachers perform their roles according to the professional model. This kind of organisation and atmosphere has, of course, much in common with Bernstein's (1967) model of the 'open school' towards which, it appears, societal changes and educational reorganisations are moving us. His description of the 'open school' emphasises its non-bureaucratic structure, its variation of beliefs and attitudes to knowledge, its flexible organisation and the achieved roles of teacher and pupils based on cooperation. The implications of Bernstein's analysis have led him to propose an educational knowledge code which constitutes, in general, a vital guide to educational innovation and, in particular, points to the movement away from separate academic disciplines and towards curriculum integration and collaborative teaching approaches. Some of the likely developments which he suggests as a result of his analysis may be summarised as:

(a) a weakening of the boundaries between staff and students and a consequential change in the pattern of working relationships in schools;
(b) a change in attitude towards the structure of knowledge and related restructuring of flexible teaching groupings;
(c) a shift from pedagogy concerned with the learning of standard operations to one emphasising the relevance of principles;
(d) a lowering of the barriers between school and the outside world.

If the move towards a more 'open' type of school system

is presumed to be beneficial, especially with respect to opportunities for curriculum renewal, there are certain problems yet to be faced before it can become fully effective. In
the relatively unstructured open system, where subject boundaries are more permeable, the special subject-based authority and related status of teachers will tend to be undermined
so that teachers may increasingly find themselves more vis-
ible and assessible and regarded as being neither *an* authority nor *in* authority (and this trend, paradoxically, is apparent at a time when the democratisation of the teaching
profession with respect to planning and decision-making has
never been further advanced). If teachers consider such
changes in their status and role to be detrimental to promotion outside the classroom then the benefits of the open
system may be reduced. Another aspect of the open school
that may be a cause of concern is that related to its possible
differential effects on children coming from varied socio-
economic backgrounds. Hoyle (1971) has questioned in
particular whether lower working-class children are able to
benefit fully from a system requiring considerable self-
discipline, responsibility and decision-making from pupils
and parents.

From this review of current social and educational
influences which shape the climate in which the curriculum
is developed and renewed, we may proceed to examine the
findings of the Schools Council Inquiry into Physical
Education in Secondary Schools.

The Inquiry—a social survey

The investigation commissioned by the Schools Council was
knowingly conceived as a broad-based and generalised social
survey of the physical education curriculum in secondary
schools and of the teachers who were responsible for it. It
represents, therefore, a contribution to the sociology of the
physical education curriculum but because of its wide scope
it is subject to the limitations of such studies relying on
relatively gross data-analyses. A current methodological
trend in the sociological analysis of the curriculum em-

phasises an intense phenomenological approach involving relatively small samples of individuals. Such phenomenological approaches, which are concerned with the *processes* involved in the curriculum rather than its gross structure, have hardly touched the physical education curriculum; and indeed without the wide and reasonably authoritative descriptive background for reference it is difficult to see how such action-oriented approaches focusing on individual encounters could be understood or interpreted outside their special context. The Inquiry may, therefore, be considered as supplying the structural description of curriculum organisation in England and Wales, the dynamic functioning of which may be subsequently revealed by less global (i.e. phenomenological) probes.

Although the Inquiry had some very specific purposes the information collected in the survey of 575 schools went beyond the limits set by the original terms of reference (Inquiry p. 1 for terms of reference). This course of action became necessary as soon as preliminary interviews with the practising teachers were organised. The planners had conceived the schedule of required information (with a view to planning a curriculum development project) but the teachers made it clear at interview that the schedule would have more meaning and relevance if elaborated to include additional items. As a result, a great deal of information was collected and categorised into convenient descriptive 'chunks' for the purposes of the official report, though other equally appropriate arrangements of the findings are certainly possible. For the present purposes it is proposed to consider the evidence reported in the Inquiry under four headings:

(1) Objectives
(2) The teaching context
(3) Evaluation
(4) The teachers

This categorisation is proposed since it contains the main elements popularly found in prescriptions for rational curriculum planning.

(1) Objectives

The classical approach to curriculum planning following the lead set by Tyler (1949) involved the organisation of appropriate means to achieve a set of educational or learning ends. This means-to-ends perspective has recently come in for a great deal of criticism, especially in the form in which the ends are seen as a precise set of behavioural objectives (along the line advocated by Bloom (1965), Krathwohl (1964) and Mager (1962)) and the means as an inflexible programme of learning experiences. The main line of the criticism has been that curricula are not in fact planned in this way and that teachers do not pre-specify their ends according to any very organised or precise system. Indeed, Taylor (1970) in a recent operational research of teachers' approach to the curriculum gave support to this contention. It does seem unlikely that many teachers consciously and systematically set down their ends or short-term objectives and then work backwards to the planning of appropriate learning experiences. Some have tried and have found the exercise thoroughly demanding and where, in the area of physical education, behavioural objectives have been attempted, serious, if not insuperable, difficulties have been experienced. Nevertheless, one should be hesitant in coming to the conclusion that because this degree of precision is difficult the attempt at rational planning should be abandoned. Clearly, some form of rational planning must be undertaken since without some idea of his intended direction a teacher must necessarily be at a loss concerning the choice of curriculum content and teaching approach. The approach which proceeds from the starting point 'Let's try this and see what happens' may make for an interesting experiment but the resulting activity can only be rationally judged as a means to some specifiable and appropriate curriculum ends. How general or specific the teacher can be or may wish to be about ends or objectives may properly vary from situation to situation. The acceptance of a form of rational planning in which ends or objectives have a logical priority does not necessarily commit one to the doctrine of the behavioural categorisation of objectives. There are many ways of giving reasonable clarity to outcomes; but without some identifiable intentions towards which related learning experiences are planned it seems unlikely that teachers can make any progress towards an understanding of the educational process.

Even if teachers of physical education wished to specify in precise behavioural details their general curriculum and particular teaching objectives, they would be faced with special difficulties. While Bloom (1965) and his colleagues have prepared elaborate guidelines for the behavioural classification of the cognitive and affective objectives, no definitive scheme for the psychomotor domain, which is of central importance to the physical educationist, has yet emerged. However, one serious, large-scale attempt to plan and operate the physical education curriculum from the starting point of objectives set down in behavioural terms is currently under experimental scrutiny at Battle Creek, Michigan, and reports are anticipated with interest. Another difficulty for the physical education teacher interested in planning from ends to means is the confused state of the literature in this curriculum area with respect to what are considered to be worthwhile immediate and long-term objectives. An extensive search of the literature during the Schools Council Inquiry revealed a variegated list of purposes for the physical education programme ranging from relatively specific psychomotor objectives to the most broad-based and general educational aims. The nine most often mentioned objectives in the literature were assembled in

TABLE 3.1   OBJECTIVES OF THE PHYSICAL EDUCATION PROGRAMME

Rank for Men		Rank for Women
6	Emotional stability	3
3	Self-realisation	2
1	Leisure-time pursuits	4
7	Social competence	6
5	Moral development	5
4	Organic development	8
2	Motor skills	1
9	Aesthetic appreciation	9
8	Cognitive development	7

random order (Table 3.1) and the teachers were asked to rank them in order from 1 (highest) to 9 (lowest).

The men teachers rate most highly the objectives leisure-time pursuits, motor skills and self-realisation and gave their lowest ratings to cognitive development and aesthetic appreciation. Women teachers rated highest motor skills, self-realisation and emotional development and gave the lowest positions to cognitive development, organic development and aesthetic appreciation. Both groups put moral development in the fifth or middle-ranked position. There was, therefore, reasonable agreement among the men and women physical educationists as to the priority they attached to these objectives but enough interesting differences were revealed to encourage further study of these general findings. There is also some evidence here to indicate that women teachers, compared with their men colleagues, are inclined to be more concerned with long-term and broad-based educational outcomes (e.g. self-realisation and emotional stability) and less concerned with the more traditional and specific objective of physical fitness (or organic development). Further analyses carried out revealed that there were some important (possibly related) differences in the ranking of these objectives according to the age of the teachers (Inquiry, p. 37). Younger teachers (men and women) tended to give more importance to the broader educational objectives—emotional stability, social competence and cognitive development—than did older teachers. Together these analyses by sex and age may be indicative of a tendency for younger teachers in general and women teachers in particular to have broader and more 'open' perspectives on their educational contributions. This in turn may reflect newer and less subject-bound approaches to the education and training of physical education teachers in general but especially of women teachers. If this is so it would represent the first and most important move towards curriculum renewal. Certainly there are some signs here that physical education teachers are currently considering objectives of their teaching programmes that are neither according to traditional expectations nor narrowly conceived. As we shall see later in this chapter, there is additional evidence to support this notion in that the same teachers see the effects of their programme to be as much social as physical. (There is a related and interesting suggestion from Taylor (1973) that the objectives of physical education as represented in the Inquiry indicate a shifting of values towards the 'self' e.g. self-realisation, aesthetic, moral and away from group and shared concerns which is not altogether in line with the present interpretation.)

Of course, whether or not objectives based on teachers' (or anyone else's) opinions are right or are the best or are the most desirable is another matter. Mostly teachers' choices and decisions are based on value judgments as Hirst (1969) has forcibly argued. Rational choice of objectives requires a defence on philosophical, psychological, social, practical or other grounds and will involve, therefore, something more than the bland acceptance of statements and opinions of teachers and pupils. In fact, and not surprisingly, it was found during the interviews with some of the teachers that the consideration of precise objectives did not constitute a large part of their curriculum planning. Their major concern appeared to be the teaching context and in particular the methods and content to be used.

(2) *The teaching context*

The Inquiry provided a great deal of information concerning the methods and content in physical education. In this section some of the evidence is collated and interpreted under Taylor's (1970) operational description, the Teaching Context, which for the present purposes takes in:

    (i) the selection and sequencing of the subject content;
    (ii) the teaching methods and strategies to be employed; and
    (iii) the consideration of factors which may influence the teachers' effectiveness.

(*i*) *Content and sequencing*

For many years now the purpose and content of physical

education has been treated as 'problematic' in the sense that teachers have worked less and less according to the prescriptions of external experts and advisers and more on the basis of their own values and judgments of what appeared to be most appropriate. The 'new sociology' would no doubt give coherence and meaning to the different perspectives and choices of teachers with respect to curriculum content by collecting evidence via action-oriented researches. Such an undertaking would need to be formidable if it were to sample the known range of teachers' content decisions. The Inquiry approach was necessarily general and global and reduced the physical education curriculum content to a simple list of activities assembled from the literature and direct observation. Most physical education teachers would perhaps tend to argue that the activities themselves are of less importance than the ways in which they are used as process vehicles for educational outcomes. Nevertheless, the activities are important in identifying the special educational area occupied by physical education.

Thirty-five single activities regularly found in current programmes were listed and sub-divided into six groups of related activities categorised as gymnastics, swimming, athletics, dance, outdoor pursuits and team games.

Figures 3.2 and 3.3 show the relative emphasis (emphasis was interpreted in the Inquiry as the time allocated to a

Rank	Activity	Year				
		1	2	3	4	5
1	Team games					
2	Gymnastics					
3	Athletics					
4	Swimming					
5	O/D pursuits					
6	Dance					

Figure 3.2   Activity emphasis: boys

Rank	Activity	Year				
		1	2	3	4	5
1	Team games	➡	➡	➡	➡	➡
2	Gymnastics	┈⟶	┈⟶	┈⟶	┈⟶	┈⟶
3	Swimming	───	⟶	⟶	⟶	⟶
4	Athletics	───	╌╌⟶	───╌	─╌─⟶	─╌─⟶
5	Dance	─╌─⟶	─╌─⟶	─╌╌	╌╌⟶	───⟶
6	O/D pursuits	⟹	⟹	⟹	⟹	⟹

Figure 3.3   Activity emphasis: girls

group of activities) placed on these groups of activities in the first five years of secondary schooling for boys and girls in England and Wales. A number of interesting findings are revealed. In the first place the over-riding importance of team games in curricula for boys and girls is emphasised throughout. This is perhaps not surprising having in mind our national games-playing heritage, though recent writings on physical education might have given the impression that team games were both losing their general appeal and were contributing less to the over-all physical education pro-gramme. Another point of note is the high emphasis given to gymnastics of one sort or another in girls' schools through-out the years under review and in boys' schools at least till the end of the third year. The moderate emphasis placed on athletics and swimming for both boys and girls is in line with commonly observed practice as is the increasing emphasis on dance for girls in the later years. In general, however, the small amount of relative change in emphasis over the years on the curriculum sub-areas is somewhat surprising and would give the impression of a rather static content reflect-ing in turn perhaps a low level of activity in curriculum renewal. Fortunately there are some local exceptions—as reported in Chapter 6.

In considering further the content or subject-matter of physical education as 'problematic' the Inquiry evidence gives some insight into what teachers actually do and where they give their emphasis. One of the main areas of speculation in recent years relates to the existence of a core of identifiable subject-matter regarded as of central importance and not as an aspect of education emanating from involvement in an aggregation of skills. Figures 3.2 and 3.3 show the continuing concern of teachers with ensuring children's involvement in games and presumably the related importance of their skills development in the programme. The teachers' commitment to gymnastics is, however, nearly as impressive for at least the first three years in the secondary school. If 'gymnastics' were here to be translated as 'educational gymnastics' the interpretation would be that teachers give substantial time to teaching general principles of movement as a core study in physical education. Some support for this line of thinking is given elsewhere in the Inquiry where it is reported that more than 90 per cent of all teachers regularly teach (some form of) gymnastics. It seems, therefore, that in attempting to define the physical education curriculum content in terms of what the teachers do, the evidence suggests that the main ingredients may be a mixture of *general* movement education (through educational gymnastics) and *specific* skills. In this sense both the earlier speculations are correct.

Teachers' content-emphasis provides no direct evidence concerning the usefulness of the concept of 'boundary' in revealing the nature of physical education. Clearly boys' departments don't emphasise dance but whether they tend to exclude it is another matter. There is some evidence, though not a lot, to suggest that the boundary between dance and the other components of the programme is weaker in girls' departments than in boys but that is hardly surprising. To stretch the findings summarised in Figures 3.2 and 3.3 to even further interpretations might allow a distinction to be drawn between aesthetic and competitive boundaries. The boys' programme (Figure 3.2) appears to be characterised by an increasing emphasis on competitive values (team games, athletics and swimming) whereas the growing importance of gymnastics and dance in the girls' programme suggests an aesthetic bias.

Some indication of a tendency to show 'open' characteristics in the later years of secondary school curriculum content are evident in the Inquiry (p. 43 and p. 52). Two pieces of information are offered in support of this notion. Firstly, it was found that the number of activities constituting the yearly programmes increased gradually over the years—more so for boys than for girls. The second and related finding was that the pupils were offered an increasing opportunity to choose activities for their programme and indeed in some schools were given the option of not taking part at all! For the purpose of the Inquiry three types of school programme were categorised: 'compulsory'—where attendance was required and no choice of activities was given; 'compulsory with choice'—where attendance was compulsory but a choice of activities was available; 'optional'—where attendance was not required but encouraged and a choice of activity was available. In about 65 per cent of the schools there was a compulsory programme in the first year but less than 5 per cent of them had this kind of programme in the fifth year and only 1 per cent in the sixth form years.

(ii) Teaching methods and strategies

Esland (1971) has suggested that questions related to the analysis of pedagogy might be conveniently organised into three groups concerned with (a) the child's ability; (b) teaching style; and (c) learning. Traditionally, the physical educationist has not overtly made assumptions concerning the pupils' ability to benefit from the physical education programme, nor has there been any strong indication that teaching methodology varies according to the intellectual status of normal children. Nevertheless, the high academic achievers occupy more places on school representative teams than do low achievers (McIntosh, 1966). Whether this is explainable in terms either of covert teacher-behaviour favouring the academically bright child or of the high attrition rate of the less-bright, or whether other factors are responsible, is not known. Certainly the process involved would be susceptible to a phenomenological approach of the sort favoured by the action-oriented sociologists. Unfortunately, the Inquiry gave no obvious evidence directly relevant to this pedagogical issue. It did, however, provide some useful information about aspects of the other two which Esland categorises as 'teaching styles' and 'learning' though for the present purposes interpretations of the findings concerning teaching styles are emphasised.

Methods and styles of teaching may vary according to the demands of different parts of the programme or according to intended outcomes. Any attempt, therefore, to characterise a teacher as having a particular style of teaching is probably ill-advised. It is, however, likely that teachers tend to use a particular style more than another. The Inquiry reports on the reaction of the teachers concerned; it estimates how often they used teaching styles described as 'direct', 'guided-discovery', 'problem-solving' and 'creative' (p. 47). It is possible to consider these styles as forming a continuum running from a relatively teacher-dominated didactic approach (direct) to a relatively unstructured learning arrangement controlled essentially by the pupils' initiative and insights (creative). The intermediary stages, guided-discovery and problem-solving, represent finer gradations from more to less teacher-involvement. Clearly this suggested continuum may be interpreted in terms of the closed-to-open concept where the teacher dominated 'direct' teaching style is at the closed end and the 'creative' style at the opposite open end. The Inquiry findings were that, in general, women teachers prefer guided-discovery and problem-solving approaches, while men teachers apparently use the direct and guided-discovery teaching styles most often. The mean scores for the two groups of teachers for each of the

TABLE 3.2   STYLES OF TEACHING—MEAN SCORES

	Style	Mean—Men	Mean—Women
Closed	Direct	3·80	3·41
↓	Guided Discovery	3·72	4·17
	Problem Solving	3·29	3·72
Open	Creative	2·32	2·77

Note: Rating Scale (see Inquiry p. 78)
1—Never; 2—Seldom; 3—Occasionally; 4—Often; 5—Great

four teaching approaches (summarised in Table 3.2) seem to indicate a more open attitude among the women.

When the teaching styles were compared according to the age of the teachers, it was found that the younger teachers were attracted less to the direct (closed) teacher-dominated methods and more to the open methods in which there was a substantial involvement of the pupils. In summary, therefore, it would seem that:

(a) the profession may be said to make differential use of teaching styles ranging from those reflecting a fairly open approach to those describing a structured and closed approach; and

(b) the profile of women and younger teachers appears to demonstrate a stronger commitment to open and less-structured styles.

These findings are hardly surprising. Younger teachers will no doubt be reflecting in their teaching styles current experimentation with a variety of relatively 'open' classroom approaches and women physical educationists may well be more affected than men by the stylistic opportunities afforded by the freer, more fluid and less-structured situations in, for example, dance and educational gymnastics. Indeed, the Inquiry gave some evidence which supports this point (p. 48). Whereas in the teaching of gymnastics the women teachers are reported to rely mostly on 'movement principles' (e.g. time, weight, space) which provide for flexibility in planning and teaching, the men give highest priority to 'lead-up stages' which, by definition, emphasise pre-structured strategy. In doing so men teachers may be reflecting implicit assumptions not only about the *way* of teaching gymnastics but also about the *nature* of this 'core' area of the physical education programme. It might be interpreted, for instance, that the relative importance of 'lead-up stages' for men teachers is indicative of their skills-oriented approach to the teaching of gymnastics and to the way they assume children will best learn such skills.

(iii) Factors influencing teacher effectiveness

There are, of course, many factors outside the realm of curriculum planning which may affect the teacher in carrying out his intentions. Taylor (1974) has indeed distinguished between the 'intended curriculum' and the 'operational curriculum'—the first describing the guide or plan (of the skills, knowledge attitudes and values) which the school or the teacher would wish to pursue and the second describing the *de facto* curriculum which is actually taught. Influences and constraints on the curriculum may work in a variety of ways and may, for example, be taken to include such general effects as the prevailing attitudes and atmosphere in the school, the resources available and the number and diversity of the pupils as well as the more specific interpersonal teacher–pupil relationships. In the rationale to a recent study of these factors which shape the operational curriculum in the primary school, Taylor (1974) summarised the problem as follows:

> What is taught is in the end conveyed in a set of transactions, called teaching, between teachers and children. Both the form and content of these transactions can be modified and restricted by physical, ideological and personal constraints and influences. What these constraints and influences are, how they operate, the extent to which they function as systems or sub-systems, their relative strength—these are the questions which this study sets out to explore.

Such factors as these constitute a vital part of the social context in which the curriculum operates and deserve the closest attention by those interested in the processes by which the curriculum is modified intentionally and unintentionally. The Inquiry attempted to describe the relatively superficial dimensions of the influences and constraints affecting the physical education teacher as a starting point from which further detailed case studies of the *process* might develop (p. 26). The teachers were asked to rate in terms of 'importance' twenty items, derived from interviews and the literature, which it was thought might be expected to have a widespread effect on the teachers' operations and over which they might be considered to have little or no control. In the highest ranked position (and, therefore, the most important) were items described as 'adequacy of facilities', 'timetable allocation', 'freedom to experiment' and 'timetable load'. When the responses to the items were intercorrelated and a component analysis undertaken to identify the major dimensions explaining the teachers reactions to these items, seven factors in order of size were described as follows:

(a) total work commitment;
(b) diversity of students;
(c) resources;
(d) liberal atmosphere;
(e) safety;
(f) attitude of colleagues;
(g) discipline.

While influences, such as the attitude of 'other subject' colleagues and the innovative (liberal) atmosphere generated presumably by the head teacher, are acknowledged in this analysis, it is the *constraints* that assume the greatest importance and constitute the three largest factors. The physical education teachers put 'total work commitment' as the factor most likely to reduce their effectiveness, which presumably reflects their view of the work load constituted of both formal curriculum teaching and the extra-curriculum duties. This constraint as perceived by the teachers may be a more vital limiting factor on the intended than on the operational curriculum. Its emphasis in this analysis would certainly also support the constantly reported concern of physical educationists with the generalised assumptions that they should accept responsibility for extra curriculum work such as team coaching, inter-school matches, camps and expeditions. The second factor, 'diversity of students', is another constraint which might be peculiar to physical education teachers in so far as they tend to be confronted with classes of widely varying physical abilities. The third factor, in order of importance, refers to a more predictable and generalised area of concern among teachers, namely, the limiting effect on the planned curriculum of lack of the appropriate resources. The expectations of teachers with respect to the resources (e.g. facilities and equipment) that they feel should be available may be linked in some way with their professional preparation, their commitment to innovative programmes and even to their age. In a further analysis of the Inquiry data it was found that women physical educationists and the younger teacher of both sexes rated the 'Resources' factor significantly higher than their other colleagues. The expectations of younger teachers and their commitment to innovation emanating from their more recent and 'open' professional preparation might understandably explain their higher concern with resources than older teachers, but the finding that women physical educationists rate this factor higher than men in general is not easy to explain. Only further in-depth study would reveal the nature of any real difference.

This analysis of factors seen by the teachers as affecting them in their effort to carry out their curriculum plans should be taken as no more than a preliminary essay into the dynamics of the social context in which the curriculum operates. There are clear indications here, however, of what further action-oriented studies will reveal about teachers' attitudes, perceptions, roles and expectations, which together represent powerful influences on the operational curriculum.

(3) Evaluation

Increasing emphasis is being placed by theorists and practitioners alike on the need to evaluate outcomes of teaching programmes. In a rational approach this will require the initial establishment of criteria by which the knowledge, skills and values, which it is intended pupils should acquire, are to be assessed—whether by written test, objective examination or teacher rating. Whether the planning emphasises intended outcomes or the *post hoc* assessment of unintended outcomes, the criteria for evaluation ought to be made explicit if they are to have any useful meaning in estimating the effects of courses. In physical education the problems of evaluation in certain aspects of the programme are minimal as, for example, in the assessment of organic fitness; but with respect to proposed emotional, social and aesthetic outcomes the difficulties of evaluation are considerable. Moreover, it seems likely that where teachers are concerned at all with such general and relatively imprecise outcomes they make judgments based mostly on their personal philosophy and perceptions. The Inquiry investigated some aspects of these perceptions through the process of asking the teachers to indicate what they considered to be the effects on their pupils of the physical education programme (p. 55). From a list of thirty possible effects they gave greatest importance to such single outcomes as 'enjoyment of participation', 'release from tension', 'general self-confidence' and 'general physical development'. It was not until a more detailed analysis was carried out (which demonstrated the pattern of association between the listed effects) that the meaning of the teachers' perceptions of the effects of their teaching could be interpreted. The further factorial analysis makes it possible to suggest that physical education teachers may see the effects of their work as being in the following broad areas which are listed in order of importance:

(a) social awareness and responsibility;
(b) general physical development;
(c) self-awareness;
(d) general movement ability;
(e) general interest in school;
(f) enjoyment in physical activity;
(g) cognitive judgment.

It is perhaps somewhat surprising to find that the teachers perceived the most important outcome of their programmes to be the development of their pupils' social awareness and responsibility. If this is so, then the perceived function and role of the physical education teacher may have changed a great deal in recent years and deserves closer investigation. The predominance of social outcomes over the general physical development effects is especially interesting and, having in mind the continuing emphasis on team games in school programmes, it might seem that games-playing is considered by teachers as a vehicle for socialisation (rather than physical development) in a more positive way than we have been led to believe. This Inquiry analysis and interpretation is offered as no more than a tentative contribution to the understanding of teachers' perceptions of the effects of their teaching, and further corroboration is needed before curriculum-planning decisions are made on the basis of this finding. Nevertheless, there is here clearer and more objective evidence, than has so far been reported, of teachers' emphatic concern about the social outcomes of physical education. Whether or not physical education does significantly affect the development of social awareness and responsibilities is, of course, another unresolved question. It may well be that, as a result of the attention directed by the Inquiry towards the perceived primacy of social outcomes, curriculum researchers and others may be attracted to the fascinating and critically important issues raised by these findings.

Although the Inquiry was not structured with this in mind, it is interesting to compare the teachers' ratings of the *objectives* (Table 3.1, p. 78) with their perception of the *effects* of the physical education programme. There is apparently some congruence, as one might expect, between intentions and outcomes. The three effects identified above as (b)—general physical development, (c)—self-awareness and (d)—general movement ability may presumably correspond to the highly-rated objectives—motor skills, leisure pursuits and self-realisation. However, there is clearly not much agreement between objectives and effects with respect to the social issue. Whereas social awareness and responsibility is represented as the most important outcome the objective listed as social competence, which may be taken to be roughly equivalent, is given a relatively low rating by the teachers.

(4) The teachers

In the last analysis the individual teacher in his idiosyncratic way manipulates and produces the operational curriculum.

His in-built and developed attitudes and personal characteristics may be expected to influence, to some extent, the shape
of the curriculum that he plans and eventually teaches. Such
personal resources may have an even greater effect on the
approach to curriculum innovation. The possibility that physical educationists are, in personal disposition, somewhat
different from other teachers has been suggested from time
to time and if this were so we might perhaps anticipate
consequential effects on the physical education curriculum.
Unfortunately, there is little or no rigorous evidence that
physical educationists differ from other teachers in terms of
such potentially interesting variables as I.Q., extraversion,
integrity, creativity, authoritarianism and innovativeness.
The Inquiry, however, included a short questionnaire of
twenty-four items describing personal characteristics considered to be of some importance for teachers in general (p.
29). The questionnaire was based on items used in Miller's
(1971) ATO Enquiry: *Students Becoming Teachers.* The
questionnaire was introduced by the question, 'How important for a successful teacher of physical education do you
consider each of the following items?' Highly ranked items
referred to the 'ideal' teacher's ability to inspire and communicate with the pupils and to his personal integrity and
knowledge. The lowest-ranked item was 'family background
in teaching'—which is not without some sociological significance! When the teachers' ratings were further analysed to
investigate the major explanatory characteristics the following seven factors, in order of their importance, were identified:

(a) personal education;
(b) social concern;
(c) rapport;
(d) knowledge of children;
(e) professional organisation;
(f) assurance;
(g) application.

The 'ideal' physical educationist was accordingly seen by the
profession as having a profile with positive and high scores

on these seven factors. To the extent that these physical education teachers rate 'personal education' (i.e. a good academic record) highest they react in the same way as *general* student teachers (Miller, 1971). The second factor, 'social concern', may be peculiar to physical educationists, reflecting their real or idealised view of the altruistic and socially sensitive nature of the teachers' function. The presence of this 'social' factor as an important characteristic of successful teachers is congruent with the finding, reported on p. 90, that 'social awareness and responsibility' was held by teachers to be the single most important effect of physical education. The third factor, 'rapport', emphasises the need in the 'ideal' teacher for those personal qualities which would give rise to 'open' interpersonal relationships, especially with pupils, which are popularly regarded as essential for the successful physical educationist. The other four characteristics listed are those which might perhaps be expected as general dispositions for successful teachers in any subject.

In general then it would appear that, if these teachers' perceptions are reasonably accurate, the admired characteristics typifying the successful physical educationist may be those of social concern and interpersonal communicating ability. These two characteristics may distinguish the physical educationist from other teachers and may, in turn, create a psychological 'set' which physical educationists bring to curriculum planning and expected outcomes.

Beyond the Inquiry

The Inquiry was clearly intended to be no more than a beginning to an assessment and possible renewal of the physical education curriculum in secondary schools. It was in fact a broad-based social survey which had as its purpose a description of the structure and operation of the curriculum as seen by the teachers. Because of the size and nature of the enterprise, it inevitably invites the criticisms often applied to 'systems-oriented' approaches which report the relevant findings as summary abstract statistics. But how else is the broad framework to be revealed? And without such a framework there are no reference points for further intensive 'action-oriented' studies. For too long the study and development of the physical education curriculum has relied on anecdotes, impressions and instincts of what was and what might be appropriate, the teachers being re-assured, in the last analysis by their undoubted dedication. But as Taylor (1974) has put it:

> Teachers need to play their part by recognising that the first essentials of professionalism lie not in dedication—which, though it may be a requirement of entry to the profession is not the substance of its competence—but in understanding the job.

The Inquiry has contributed to our knowledge and under-standing of the job of teaching physical education in secondary schools and has revealed something of the teachers' values, the perceptions of their contributions and the constraints under which they work. The purpose of this chapter has been to interpret this information in the social context of current curriculum reform. At the very least physical education teachers and the profession at large will now be better informed of the factors shaping present-day physical education so that such influences and procedures once identified may be assessed, challenged and perhaps changed. But the study of the physical education curriculum must go a lot further. The Inquiry and the present elaboration is only an enticing foretaste of what more detailed studies will unfold about the plans and practices, the roles and relationships, the ideas, values and expectations that are essential elements of the curriculum process.

The Inquiry had, of course, the main purpose of providing the basis for a curriculum development project. Indeed it has given rise to a number of proposals which in their different ways would surely give a needed impetus to curriculum renewal. Apart from the necessarily parochial curriculum experiments that are proceeding, with modest resources, in a few centres in England, there would seem to be a need for a larger and more embracing project with the resources available to make an impact on the teaching of physical education comparable to that made by recent Schools Council Projects on, for example, the teaching of mathematics and languages.

References

BERNSTEIN, B. (1967) 'Open schools, open society?' *New Society* **10**, 259–69.

BLOOM, B. S. *et al.* (1965) *Taxonomy of Educational Objectives: Handbook 1: The Cognitive Domain.* Longman: London.

CORWIN, R. G. (1965) *A Sociology of Education.* Appleton-Century-Crofts: New York.

ESLAND, G. H. (1971) 'Teaching and learning as the organisation of knowledge' in YOUNG, M. (ed.) *Knowledge and Control.* Collier-Macmillan: London.

HALPIN, A. W. (1967) 'Change and Organisational Climate'. *Journal of Educational Administration* **5**, 1.

HIRST, P. H. (1969) 'The logic of the curriculum'. *Journal of Curriculum Studies* **1**, 2.

HOYLE, E. (1971) 'How does the curriculum change?' in HOOPER, R. (ed.) *The Curriculum: Context, Design and Development.* Oliver and Boyd: Edinburgh.

KANE, J. E. (1974) *Physical Education in Secondary Schools.* Schools Council Research Studies. Macmillan: London.

KRATHWOHL, D. R. *et al.* (1964) *Taxonomy of Educational Objectives: Handbook 2: The Affective Domain.* Longman: London.

MCINTOSH, P. C. (1966) 'Mental ability and success in sport'. *Research in Physical Education* **1**, 15.

MAGER, R. F. (1962) *Preparing Instructional Objectives.* Fearon Publishers: Chicago.

MILLER, G. W. (1971) *Students Becoming Teachers.* ATO Enquiry Report. University of London Institute of Education: London.

MILES, M. B. (1964) *Innovation in Education.* Teachers' College, Columbia University: New York.

TAYLOR, P. H. (1970) *How Teachers Plan their Courses.* Studies in Curriculum Planning. Eyre and Spottiswoode for NFER: London.

TAYLOR, P. H. (1973) 'Curricula in Transition: the case of Physical Education'. *Studies in Physical Education.* ATCDE: London.

TAYLOR, P. H. *et al.* (1974) *Purpose, Power and Constraint in the Primary School Curriculum.* Schools Council Research Studies. Macmillan: London.

CHAPTER FOUR

Teacher Involvement in Curriculum Planning

Leonard Almond

It would seem from the evidence of many school timetables that schools regard their curricula as fixed entities, not variable structures to be adjusted in the interests of achieving some objective. Perhaps the origin for this view lies in the Latin root of the word 'curriculum' which means 'racecourse'—and the virtue of a racecourse is that it is fixed and standard. However (to use a related image with very different connotations) the curriculum also resembles a 'race'; thus it may be seen as the *result* of constant jockeying for position as competing claims contest for places in a list of priorities. Surprisingly, year after year the result of this race remains unchanged in many schools—the curriculum unaltered, the goals the same.

Perhaps the real reason for this widespread conservatism in schools is the lack of a clear specification of the goal-selection procedure (it was Wiseman (1970) who pointed out that we lack a useful specification for this procedure—although curriculum-planners must consider it to be of outstanding importance). Faced, therefore, with a multitude of possible alternative goals, curriculum-planners—conservatives and innovators alike—are forced to make arbitrary decisions about what the curriculum shall comprise: pupils are required to study certain subjects and forbidden to study others; encouraged to pursue some topics and discouraged from pursuing others; provided with opportunities to study some phenomena and not provided with the means to study others—and yet the areas excluded may well have greater claims for inclusion than those areas actually taught. To function responsibly, therefore, the schools need a usable model on which to base their curriculum-planning decisions.

Important though such decisions are, many other vital issues need to be resolved in the planning and development of curricula: we lack, for example, a clear specification of what is involved in change and innovation. Moreover, the curriculum-planning models that have been made available to teachers have not been used by them; therefore it is clearly no good having carefully drawn up aims and objectives if they cannot be implemented. These two issues— innovation and teacher involvement—illustrate the complexity of the task facing anyone seriously interested in planning and developing curricula.

From the evidence of a number of teaching journals and the publications of the Schools Council, there appears to be a lot of activity, called 'curriculum development', in this area. Regardless of what activity is going on, or supposedly going on, there does not appear to be a clear rationale involved in this development. Without a rationale and without any understanding of the problems of curriculum policy-making, curriculum innovation and curriculum development, all this activity may be in vain.

The purpose of this chapter is to raise some of the problems created by the movement for curriculum development and to isolate certain issues that seem to be important. In order to isolate these issues this chapter is divided into five sections:

(1) Approaches to curriculum planning
(2) Innovation and change
(3) Agencies for change
(4) The changing concept of evaluation
(5) The implications of curriculum development for physical education

Rather than provide answers to these problems it is intended to provide a platform from which debate and discussion can follow. The title of this chapter, 'Teacher Involvement in

Curriculum Planning', reflects a concern for the *teacher*—who is central to the whole notion of planning and development.

(1) Approaches to curriculum planning

A central issue in curriculum theory has been the development of a rational planning model. The most persistent theoretical formulation in this area has been Ralph Tyler's now classic syllabus for 'Education 360' at the University of Chicago: *Basic Principles of Curriculum and Instruction.* Tyler wrote this book in order 'to explain a rationale for viewing, analysing, and interpreting the curriculum and instruction programme for an educational institution' (Tyler, 1949). He raises four fundamental questions, and if curriculum development is to proceed, these questions need to be answered.

- (a) What educational purposes should the school seek to attain?
- (b) What educational experiences can be provided that are likely to attain these purposes?
- (c) How can these educational experiences be effectively organised?
- (d) How can we determine whether these purposes are being attained?

'Planning by Objectives'—the behavioural approach

Tyler's questions can be reformulated into the now familiar four-stage process by which any curriculum can be developed: state your objectives, select experiences, organise these experiences, and evaluate. However, it must be made quite clear that Tyler is concerned with how a school goes about framing a chosen goal, rather than with the statement of what specific goals are in a school's best interests. As Tyler says, 'in the final analysis objectives are a matter of choice for the teachers, administrators, the programme developers—of those responsible for the school'. Consequently, Tyler develops a commitment to framing pre-specified objectives in behavioural terms.

> Since the real purpose of education is not to have the instructor perform certain activities to bring about significant changes in the students' patterns of behaviour, it becomes important to recognise that any statement of the objectives of a school should be a statement of changes to take place in students (p. 44).

In a further statement, Tyler confirms his position even more:

> The most useful form for stating objectives is to express them in terms which identify both the kind of behaviour to be developed in the student and the content or area of life in which this behaviour is to operate (p. 46).

In this context education is seen as changing behaviour in desirable directions. Objectives are translated into statements of behavioural goals, and the precise way in which behaviour is to be changed is carefully delineated. Learning experiences are planned to bring about these desirable behavioural goals. The success of these learning experiences is measured in terms of the stated behavioural goals. Thus behavioural objectives become the criteria by which content is outlined, materials selected, activities planned, teaching methods and techniques developed.

Though Tyler indicates that his rationale is but one way of viewing curriculum design, the Tyler formulation has become *the* rationale. Consequently, many curriculum developers fail to recognize that there can be other rationales. This failure may be due to the lack of accessibility of clearly formulated alternative models, but it is probably due to a lack of understanding of the nature of the curriculum.

Within the Tyler methodology there seem to be three assumptions which need questioning:

(i) that aims or goals should be expressed in behavioural terms;

(ii) that learning experiences can be selected and controlled by the teacher; and

(iii) that 'outcomes' can be evaluated in terms of 'intention achievement'.

(i) Behavioural goals

The behavioural approach to goal selection implies that teachers know their objectives prior to teaching and can specify the outcomes of teaching prior to their interaction with pupils. In many cases this will have been the result of subjecting general statements of aims to analytic scrutiny in order to derive checklists of objectives which will be used as guidelines for curriculum planning.

A typical response to this prescription is outlined by Wiseman and Pidgeon (1970) in a discussion on objectives:

> These should be set down in clear, unambiguous terms describing the expected changes in behaviour. The word behaviour is used in this context to cover all activities that can be assessed or inferred. It covers not only the acquisition of knowledge and skills, but also the development of attitudes and interests. It is the expression of objectives in terms of expected behavioural change that distinguishes them from the more general goals that might be ascribed to a course. These are more vague and more indefinite, and can be thought of more as declarations of intent than descriptions of behaviour.

The advocates of this approach also claim that behavioural objectives focus attention on the pupil's performance rather than on the teacher's. Popham (1969) writes:

> ... precise objectives stated in terms of measurable learner behaviour make it infinitely easier for the teacher to engage in curricular decisions. The clarity of precisely stated goals permits the teacher to make more judicious choices regarding what ought to be in the curriculum.

All this sounds very plausible, but a number of critics have questioned the assumptions that educational objectives should be framed in behavioural terms. One danger that critics echo consistently is that preoccupation with behavioural objectives, highlighting measurable performance, limits and distorts the range of purposes many educators would wish to advance.

Eisner (1967) believes that there are four main weaknesses in the argument for pre-specification of objectives. First: educational outcomes cannot be predicted with the accuracy claimed. Second: some subjects are not amenable to the degree of specificity required; therefore the possibility of specifying with precision will depend on the particular subject. Third: objectives could tend to be formulated for situations where performances can be measured easily, confusing the application of a standard and the making of a judgment. Fourth: he believes that in implying that the formulation of objectives should be a first step in curriculum planning, the behaviourists confuse the logical requirement of relating means to ends and the psychological conditions useful for constructing curricula. He also argues that teachers would need to spend considerable time in formulating objectives if they are to be stated in precise detail—time which is not readily available to the teacher of physical education.

Stenhouse (1971) has pointed out that the realities of the classroom situation must be taken into account and it is here, he believes, that the problems of the rational planning model arise. The complexity of the school and the classroom lies at the centre of limitations imposed by the Tyler model. He suggests that it is not enough to be logical, because teachers who assent to lists of objectives interpret them differently and synthesise them in different ways. Groups of teachers who claim to have agreed on their objectives often demonstrate in the classroom that their agreement was illusory (see also Smith and Keith, 1971). For Stenhouse, objectives are inadequate as definitions of value positions. Their analytic nature, far from clarifying and defining value divergence, appears to make it possible to mask such divergence. In practice, therefore, he believes that teachers will have difficulty in controlling a course coherently by persistent running-reference to schedules of objectives.

(ii) The selection and control of learning experiences

Tyler's second assumption rests on his notion of a learning experience. After the first step of stating objectives has been accomplished, the rationale proceeds to the stages of selecting and organizing learning experiences as the means for achieving pre-specified ends. It is difficult to see how a teacher can select learning experiences when Tyler has defined them as the interaction between a student and the environment. In this situation the learning experience will be a function of the past experience of the student, his perceptions and his inclinations, and a structured environment. Nevertheless, while Tyler can see this difficulty he believes that the teacher is able to control the learning experience through the 'manipulation of the environment in such a way as to set up stimulating situations—situations that will evoke the kind of behaviour desired' (p. 64). Is Tyler really suggesting that we manipulate pupils through the shaping of behaviour for pre-determined ends? Kleibarb (1970) objects to this approach when he points out that 'It is even questionable whether stating objectives at all, when they represent external goals allegedly reached through the manipulation of learning experiences, is a fruitful way to conceive of the process of curriculum'. Indeed, there does seem to be an urgent need for a critical analysis of the whole concept of a learning experience exemplified in the Tyler model.

(iii) The evaluation of 'outcomes'

The third assumption in this model is concerned with the nature of evaluation. According to Tyler, 'The process of evaluation is essentially the process of determining to what extent the educational objectives are actually being realised by the programme of curriculum and instruction' (p. 105). In other words the pre-specification of objectives forms the standard by which outcomes will be matched and assessed. It is this rationale which has formed the basis of almost all subsequent evaluation thought. Thus curriculum evaluation has tended to follow this classic model of curriculum planning, where evaluation is a self-corrective process of determining whether learning experiences have led to the attainment of pre-specified objectives.

However, an evaluation procedure based on this approach is unsatisfactory. The outcomes of learning are multidimensional, and evaluation should map out what all the effects of a course are. The most significant dimensions of an educational activity may be those that are completely unplanned and unanticipated. Consequently, an emphasis on one particular role of evaluation, the evaluation of intention-achievement, will tend to obscure the potential value of evaluation information.

'Planning by hypotheses'—the procedural approach

In the Tyler model with its emphasis on pre-specified outcomes and the selection of appropriate learning experiences, there seems to be a distinct danger that more emphasis will be placed on the degree of efficiency with which outcomes are achieved rather than the outcomes themselves. In short, there will be a correlation between ends and the means, rather than between ends and their consequences. A pre-specified outcomes approach emphasises not the process of creation, but rather the product. Because of this objection to the Tyler model, one must look for an alternative way of curriculum planning in physical education. Physical education is concerned with the development of physical experience through sporting activities—which provide opportunities to transform and enrich the personal life-style of an individual. In the development of this experience, the individual would have the opportunity to formulate his own purposes, act upon his own choices, and receive the consequences thereof.

An alternative approach to looking at curriculum planning has been suggested by Stenhouse (1971). Where action is disciplined by principles of procedure rather than preconceived specific outcomes, Stenhouse argues that we may do better to deal in hypotheses concerning effects rather than in objectives. The assumption of this approach is that teachers can, from their understanding of a general aim, develop effective teaching strategies. In this creative approach, outcomes are open to interpretation by particular teachers for particular pupils. By developing understanding of the ways in which a curriculum is likely to have an impact upon pupils and by taking into account the wide range of possible effects, we shall have a better basis for a more complete understanding of the complexities of a task, which, because of its familiarity, is all too often taken for granted. Only when we have a better understanding of what we can do in the teaching context will we be in a position to make proposals for change which are based on what is possible, rather than on theories, ideologies and slogans which are out of touch with the realities of the classroom.

This view is supported by Macdonald (1965) who states that our objectives are only known to us in any complete sense after the completion of our act of teaching. No matter what we thought we were attempting to do, we can only know what we wanted to accomplish after the fact. On the basis of this rationale, Macdonald suggests that objectives are heuristic devices which provide initiating sequences which may change during the process of teaching. In a similar manner Eisner (1967) writes:

> The ends achieved are not pre-conceived but reflected upon in retrospect rather than in prospect. This, I believe is what most teachers do in the process of curriculum development.

Consequently, he suggests a second type of objective which he calls an 'expressive objective'. An 'expressive objective' describes an educational encounter: it identifies a situation in which pupils are to work, a problem with which they are to cope, a task in which they are to engage; but it does not specify what they are to learn from that encounter, situation, or problem. An 'expressive objective' is evocative rather than prescriptive.

The approach suggested by Stenhouse and Eisner seems to be one in which the teacher first identifies a working situation and then, from his past experience, or from exploratory case-studies, generates hypotheses about the possible range of effects from this encounter. It provides the teacher with a vehicle through which an area of experience can be explored, and it allows pupils the opportunity to develop their own interests. However, this is not an easy option as a replacement for the Tyler model. The teacher is acting as his own researcher in an attempt to clarify his own thought and understanding about the opportunities for learning and development that he makes available for pupils. There is no substitute for clarity of thought and depth of understanding in the educational enterprise. It may be possible to achieve this, but only by constant revision and examination of our hypotheses about effects where action is disciplined by principles of procedure.

'Planning by issues', and 'planning by transactions'

Taylor (1972) has suggested that there are two further alternative models of planning open to teachers: the first one he calls 'planning by issues'. In this process of planning some teachers may question particular assumptions about the values of physical education in a school, seeing possibilities for a rethinking of certain areas of concern. For instance, it may be that some teachers would no longer consider that physical education in its present form makes a significant contribution to the health of a pupil. Such teachers would prefer to emphasise the notion of education as providing access to activities which the pupils value rather than to activities selected as being valuable by well-intentioned adults. In this context, physical education is seen as a contribution not to the health of a pupil but to his personal life-style.

The emergence of these new conceptions creates an issue which requires deliberation and action. What emerges is a platform or a base from which claims need to be argued out, justified and practical proposals for action developed and pioneered. However, what is viable in one school needs to be viable in many schools; it needs to have a direct practicality. It is here, as Taylor quite rightly points out, that 'planning by issues' meets its most difficult task: 'Many curricular issues of consequence abort after the first stage because the claims made for them in order to rally support fail to win the allegiance of the "practical man and woman", those with the capabilities essential for the implementation in the schools'. He goes on to suggest that what we should seek 'is that creative contribution from individuals which gives signifi-

cance to the plan as it affects their style of teaching, gives to
it a new direction and purpose and a new meaning to the
physical education of pupils'.

The second type of planning is 'planning by transactions',
which differs from the first because it starts in the teaching
situation, whereas 'planning by issues' has its beginning
outside the school. In this form of planning, which is closely
related to that suggested by Stenhouse, the practitioner is
seeking better proposals for practice than those he now
works by. The teacher wants access to new teaching
strategies which will have ready application to his own
situation.

> It is this way that groups of teachers given encouragement but largely
> left to follow their instincts will operate to plan new curricula at the
> transactional level. Their insights may lack sophisticated formulation
> but they are insights of both close experience and related to
> institutional constraints. The practitioner may well break new ground
> in the school long before the theorist. (Taylor, 1972)

He is trying to develop more understanding of what he is
doing and what he is not doing in the teaching context. In
this form of planning the teacher once more takes research
attitudes into the teaching situation where he reports information about reality, reality as perceived by the teacher.

Summary

Therefore, from this description and review of alternative
types of planning, there seem to be three stages of operations. The first is 'planning by issues'; once teachers have
been immersed in this process they can tackle stage two. In
stage two a teacher can either plan his courses by reference
to 'planning by objectives' (using the Tyler model), or he can
use 'planning by hypotheses' (the Stenhouse alternative). In
order to support stage two planning, teachers would benefit
from information gained in stage three, 'planning by transactions'. It is these three stages of planning that need urgent
development in physical education, but such prescriptions
require support from the teacher. It is here that the teacher

needs new skills, new competences, and a new role; but how can the physical education profession develop these?

(2) Innovation and change

It is beyond the scope of this paper to present a detailed analysis of the issues involved in curriculum innovation. However, it is important to review some of the main lessons that can be derived from experience with educational change—which illustrate the effects of innovation on the teacher and on his involvement with curriculum development.

In *The Culture of the School and the Problem of Change*, Sarason (1971) draws on his numerous experiences with curriculum innovation in order to formulate and to identify key aspects of what he calls 'the modal process of change' or the usual way in which change is introduced into the school culture. Sarason criticises curriculum innovators for trying to make innovations teacher-proof. He believes that there is a tendency to view teachers as resistant, incapable or unwilling to change, and to ignore the possibility that teachers' inadequacies in knowledge, understanding and skills are partly a result of their not having had the opportunity to develop these competencies in their past and present social situations. The question may not be whether teachers are currently capable of innovation, but whether they would develop this capacity if the situation were altered to support such development.

For the teacher, innovation has meant that they have been asked to learn procedures, vocabulary, and concepts that are not only new but likely to conflict with highly-overlearned attitudes and ways of thinking. Due to lack of sensitivity to their plight, teachers in this situation have been given little opportunity to voice uncertainties or lack of understanding; and the experts (whose theories have failed to face the problem of how one reaches one's goals) appear to believe that the introduction of new curricula involves no more than just 'development and delivery'.

Sarason warns the teacher that there is a tendency for

innovations to become ends in themselves, neglecting the intended consequences of the proposed change. Innovation must be seen as one possibility from a multitude of alternative means. If the innovation is considered to be an improvement on what already exists, it must not be assumed that it should therefore be spread as widely as possible: a strategy that is successful in one school may not be as effective in another school with different conditions.

Goodlad and Klein (1970) in their study of how educational innovations were finding their way into the classroom came up with the suggestion that highly publicised and recommended innovations of the past decade were dimly conceived and only partially implemented. They attributed the lack of real change to two factors:

(a) In an innovative setting teachers are usually only exposed to ideas. Consequently, when they are left on their own, they find that they have not internalised the full meaning of these ideas. As a result, it is not surprising that there appears to be a gap between what they think they are doing and what the authors actually observed them doing.

(b) When innovation requires a change in teaching behaviour it is unreasonable to assume that this can be accomplished by attending course lectures, participating in brief orientation sessions, reading manuals or even attending a course where the tutor talks about, rather than demonstrates new procedures. To change the pattern of teaching behaviour is a formidable task when the existing pattern has been learned in a long sequence of schooling.

In their case study of innovative practice, Smith and Keith (1971) studied an attempt by an innovatory principal to create a new curriculum using teachers selected by him for this project because they sought opportunity to do something new with the curriculum. The story of this experience with change was one of frustration and failure. At the end of the first year only eight teachers out of eighteen wished to return for the second year, and in the middle of the second year the principal left the school to take another job.

The reasons for this failure can be summed up in terms of the lack of attention to the process of implementation of pre-specified plans, and to the problem of learning new roles on the part of teachers. The main problem was that teachers were not able to work out the operational implications of formal statements of goals, which included an organisational plan and structure. Even though there was general agreement among the teachers on the desirability of the goals themselves, individually each teacher held his own views and interpretation of what the goals meant in practice, and there was no effective means of working these out together during the initial and ongoing innovation. It is quite clear that the problem arose from the tacit assumption that teachers should be capable of implementing innovations; no-one realised how much help is required in learning new roles. It was not appreciated that operational implementation of formal statements of goals requires the learning of new teaching roles and role relationships on the part of teachers; this in turn necessitates the learning of new skills and competences by teachers; and that the whole enterprise demands considerable time, opportunity and the resources for dealing with problems and issues that arise during the implementation of new curricula.

Consequently, the lesson from this study is that formal, elaborate statements of educational goals, even when they are agreed upon, are of limited value until they are linked with a means of achieving them that provides adequate support for the teacher during the process of implementation. In addition, an innovative organisation will put extra demands on those scarce and limited resources—time and energy. Innovation requires enormous energy after school, in the evenings, and at weekends.

(3) Agencies for change

In the previous section three reviews of innovatory experience illustrated the importance of the teacher and his role in curriculum development. They have important implications for retraining and supporting teachers; therefore this section is devoted to examining some agencies associated with curriculum development, and the retraining of teachers.

Centralised curriculum projects

Curriculum projects sponsored by bodies such as the Schools Council may be important as initiators, stimulating and accelerating some form of development in a particular subject area. They have been concerned mainly with developing new teaching materials in the form of a complete course, resource materials (from which teachers make selections), or teachers' guides. In many cases (e.g. Humanities Curriculum Project) this has involved teachers in adopting new teaching techniques and attitudes. A variety of methods have been used in preparing materials and ideas and promoting their use; but so far the strategy for this development has usually been to try out materials and ideas generated by a central team or 'group of experts' in trial schools and then hope that published materials will be diffused under the stimulus of conferences and in-service courses.

Subject associations

A number of subjects have set up professional associations to promote curriculum developments among their members. Through journals, newsletters and conferences they are disseminating ideas and sharing experience. In a number of cases (e.g. The Association for the Teaching of Social Science) they have established in different regions working groups of like-minded teachers who are prepared to experiment with new ideas and develop further materials. The stimulus for this work must continue to come from dedicated teachers who are prepared to put time and energy into this enterprise, despite the financial problems which are always present.

Commercial publishers

With the development of resource centres and the growing use of resource material rather than a single textbook or a series of texts, there has been a considerable increase in commercially produced material. The teacher will be faced with a vast array of very attractive material and he needs to make decisions regarding the suitability of these products for particular purposes. These materials can be helpful by providing resources which the teacher would otherwise have had to prepare. In many cases they provide support for a teacher who finds that 'planning' makes more and more demands on his time and energy.

Teachers' centres

The essence of curriculum development is involvement of teachers themselves. This means that teachers should have regular opportunities to meet together for cooperative action and thought. In Working Paper No. 10, *Curriculum Development: Teachers' Groups and Centres*, published by the Schools Council, two principles for curriculum development are outlined: first, that the motive power should come primarily from local groups of teachers accessible one to another; secondly, that there should be effective and close collaboration between teachers and all those who are able to offer support. These principles have been put into practice by the setting up of teachers' centres by local education authorities. Over 500 centres have been set up so far to assist teachers locally to respond to the demands for progress in curriculum development. Many of these centres can be described as 'general purpose' (there are also special-purpose centres providing for one kind of curriculum activity in a particular subject area). Some centres exist as 'workshops' for the production of teaching materials or the evaluation of existing resource materials. Some seek to serve as resource or information centres; others may simply serve as social centres. The success or otherwise of such centres and their impact on local development depends very much on both the degree of involvement of the centre leader and the level of support from teachers in the authority.

In-service training

The usual provision for the training of teachers for development work in schools is in-service courses in colleges of education and in education departments at universities and polytechnics. The traditional methods of instruction—lectures, seminars and tutorials—appear to be increasingly inadequate to meet the need for professional competence in curriculum development. Consequently, we are forced to change our conceptions of the nature and scale of in-service provision. A number of courses have attempted to provide alternative education for developing the skills needed for innovation and curriculum development. Among the activities employed by the personnel running such courses are the following:

    (i) Simulated activities
    (ii) Workshop courses
    (iii) Consultancy roles
    (iv) School-based curriculum development

(i) Simulated activities

Role playing, and in some cases games, are used to simulate the school situation in order to produce a model which is as close to reality as possible. A particular school, or a fictitious school which is created for a particular exercise, is set up and a brief is provided giving complete details about the school, the staff, the pupils, the facilities, and the environment. Members of the group involved in the exercise are asked to adopt certain roles in the school, and problems are introduced which the group are required to solve. In some cases these are problems of real schools, and possible solutions are fed back to the actual school for consideration. During the exercise it is possible to vary the problems and introduce additional constraints at vital decision points.

Games are an alternative form of simulated activity, but in the field of curriculum planning they are not well developed at this stage. However, they are used with some success. In this activity the players are involved in analysing problems, making decisions, and suggesting solutions which can be rewarded at different stages. The pattern of the game can be controlled and directed to introduce new problems.

The problems of using simulated activity are threefold: first, the activity can become an end in itself and, in this case, the point of the exercise is lost; second, members of the group may draw on their own experience which could be rather limited (therefore role playing needs to be supplemented by visits to schools and by seminars on issues that provide a wider perspective); finally, the simulation is only relevant in *one* situation, and it is difficult to produce a model which takes into consideration the variations in teaching patterns that exist in schools.

(*ii*) *Workshop courses*

In a workshop situation teachers can come together to discuss problems, suggest solutions, share their experience, and plan new courses. The opportunity of bringing together experienced teachers provides a valuable source for in-service education. The provision of resources and the time to reflect on one's own experience supported by the experience of other colleagues enables one to consider curriculum problems in a new light. The problems of ROSLA; a curriculum for the middle years of schooling; and an extension of existing resources for Humanities: these are some areas that a workshop can set up for examination and from which it is possible to produce workable curriculum specifications.

(*iii*) *Consultancy roles*

Very often a problem may face a teacher which is peculiar to just one school. Opportunities can be provided for a teacher to consider the problem and examine ways in which possible solutions can be considered. If the teacher is attending a course it should be possible to build this into assignments required by the course. By acting in a consultancy role a tutor can be a guide, a coordinator, a resource agent and a source of further contacts. There is no need for the tutor to be an 'expert' in every field so long as he is able to provide the opportunity for the teacher both to explore as many areas as possible and have access to contacts that can provide further insight. A number of very valuable studies have evolved from this approach and it offers considerable scope for further development. However, it creates a new role for the tutor, one where he is no longer an 'expert' but a resource coordinator and a stimulator of ideas.

(iv) School-based curriculum development

Even though teachers are provided with opportunities to attend in-service courses, much of this work tends to be away from schools. The teacher is expected to go back and involve himself in curriculum innovation and possible development. Time and energy for reflection and creative thought become a thing of the past when one is faced with the constant demands of school life. In this situation, innovation and development become difficult, and very often impossible when one is cajoled by colleagues to forget the theory and get back to the practical, 'the nitty-gritty of teaching'. Recent experience in the field of in-service education has shown that there is an element of truth in these statements. We must get down to 'the nitty-gritty of teaching' by involving not just the lucky individual who was able to secure secondment, but also his colleagues, in the practical enterprise of teacher development, and of developing curricula in the school. Why should it not be possible for in-service education to occur in the school? With the cooperation of local authorities, head teachers, and groups of interested teachers, it is possible to establish structures which enable teachers to commit themselves to in-service education, to obtain additional qualifications and be involved in on-going innovation and curriculum development without necessarily moving away from the school.

This form of activity requires a coordinator and contact man, who can provide resources and feed in ideas drawn from contacts with other schools and working groups of teachers. The practical enterprise of developing curricula can be supported by making available research reports and documents that may provide insight into the work of teachers involved in this process. The main benefit to be derived from such activity is that it involves many more teachers in in-service education.

(4) The changing concept of evaluation

In the field of evaluation studies there has been a tendency to emphasise one particular role of evaluation, the evaluation of *pupil* achievement, and this has tended to obscure the potential value of other evaluation information. However, there does not seem to be any real demand among teachers for the evaluation of their own courses. We evaluate pupils, but we never seriously consider that we should evaluate ourselves, our teaching, and the courses that we plan. We can convince ourselves that we would be overjoyed to receive data about our teaching, but when teachers are asked to involve themselves in this process a barrier suddenly appears. After all, in the teacher's eyes, what does he have to gain from having his work examined? He risks damage to his ego, and worst of all, he risks discovering that his pupils may not really care for him, or physical education. However, if we are concerned about trying to do a better job than we do at present, evaluation is an essential part of our attempt to achieve this. What kinds of evaluation data would be useful for providing feedback information that has potential value for changing our perception of the teaching role? For physical education three types of evaluation data would enable one to have a more realistic picture of the impact of physical education in schools.

(i) *Examination of intentions*
By a stringent examination of written statements of our aims, goals, or objectives, we should be able to see if we are making realistic claims about what we can achieve in physical education. A course exists primarily in the minds of teachers, yet we should communicate our intentions through some sort of course specification which is meaningful to

others: to pupils, parents, evaluators and other teachers. Only when we are clear about realistic claims in physical education can we hope to improve the quality of our teaching and have an impact on the curriculum of the school. Research has shown that there is much confusion surrounding the claims made for physical education; however, there is some indication that this may be due to the inability of some teachers to verbalise clear intentions which they can translate into meaningful teaching procedures, rather than that they have no intentions at all. Teachers do have intentions but in the process of communication this is lost. The problem, therefore, is to provide clear teaching specifications which are realistic for the teacher and the pupil. This is a major task and it must not be underestimated.

(ii) Transactional curriculum: what is actually happening?

If we have clear intentions and we are aware of what we are and are not doing in our teaching, this would be an ideal state of affairs; but this is not the case. There is very little information available about what is happening in the interaction of teacher and learner. In order to provide this information the teacher must adopt a research role. In this role the teacher is striving to develop:

(a) an awareness of what he is trying to do by reflecting upon practice and past experience;
(b) an awareness of the consequences of his teaching;
(c) an awareness of the range of possibilities that teaching can encompass—these possibilities can be restricted by choice, but very often a teacher may be unaware that other choices may be available to him;
(d) an awareness of his own performance.

The evaluation of the transactional curriculum is a concern for teacher development which is a major component of any development in the curriculum.

(iii) Input evaluation

The quality of any curriculum will depend upon sound judgments based upon timely access to valid and realistic information. In the process of formulating a curriculum many decisions have to be made; therefore a valuable source of feedback information would be lost if we did not record how decisions were made, what constraints existed, and what the reactions of other teachers and pupils were to such decisions. It is this type of information which is rarely available; yet it is such data that enables one to support and justify decisions, and make better decisions in the future. During the formulation and implementation of any course it is essential to record what decisions were made, how and why they were made.

(5) The implications of curriculum development for physical education

The planning of a curriculum does not need to involve the teachers in writing statements of preconceived, specific outcomes in the form of behavioural objectives: the teacher can adopt Stenhouse's approach which uses hypotheses about effects rather than behavioural objectives. However, it should be pointed out that the objectives movement was an attempt to achieve greater clarity and precision in the discussion of broad educational aims. By spelling out the nature of an activity, its characteristics, and disclosing the workings of an activity as ongoing processes, the objectives movement was trying to bring down to earth some of the loftier aims which educators from time to time have provided as guides to action. Therefore, both Stenhouse and the objectives movement have grounds for trying to clarify their statements of intent, their differences, and their effects.

However, physical education has a more urgent need than writing statements of objectives *in* physical education. Following Taylor's account of 'planning by issues', there seems to be a more urgent need to ask, 'What are the objectives *of* teaching physical education?' This type of question leads us into a very different area from the question, 'What are the objectives *in* teaching physical education?' In the latter, we are inside the subject with a concern for determining what sort of things a physical education teacher is trying to do. In the former, we ask the more fundamental question of how to justify physical education in the school curriculum. 'Planning by issues' is one approach that could be developed in response to this fundamental question of justification.

In the second type of planning suggested by Taylor, 'planning by transactions', the teacher is being asked to act as his own researcher providing feedback information about the realities of the teaching context. This kind of information is vital for the development of the teacher himself, his perceptions of his task, and it provides information that will reclarify declarations of intention and their subsequent translation into action.

Such plans for curriculum development need support and encouragement. Teachers' centres can provide opportunities for like-minded teachers to meet, share experiences, exchange ideas and plan cooperative action; they are also a possible source of money for supporting curriculum development. In physical education such centres seem to have been neglected and their potential ignored. Inquiries into the reasons for this neglect reveal the somewhat naïve attitude that physical education is concerned with 'action' and not talk. Talk, in the form of reflection on experience and the sharing of this experience, may provide a sounder basis for practice. Certainly, there is a need to rationalise what we are doing in physical education. In teachers' centres working groups can initiate new ideas, plan curricula, and implement joint plans for action in different settings. Within the structure of teachers' centres there is always the possibility that such working groups can form links with other centres for a further sharing of experience. If these links can be developed and extended throughout the country, we have a potential framework that could provide unity—a unity of purpose that seems to be lacking in the profession. Such hopes of unity will never be realised unless we make an attempt to plan curricula seriously.

Lectures and seminars and traditional types of courses are inadequate for developing competence in curriculum planning; therefore more appropriate in-service education needs to be devised. To meet this demand, case studies which involve practice at making decisions in simulated exercises and workshop courses have been tried with some success; nevertheless there is still a need to look further for new possibilities. Rather than go away from the school to attend courses, the place to develop competence in curriculum planning is in the school itself. Physical education teachers can draw upon the experience of colleagues in other subject areas who have been concerned with curriculum planning. By involving themselves in curriculum planning for the whole school—rather than retaining a separate identity which is common practice with physical education departments—physical education teachers will gain valuable insights into this whole process. In those schools where all the departments jointly decide upon both the general objectives of the curriculum and the specific objectives of individual subjects, a concern for the whole school curriculum by PE teachers would highlight the extent to which physical education can contribute to the education of pupils. Further support for developing curricula can be made available through contacts with experienced curriculum developers acting as advisers, who could make regular visits to the school. This is not to suggest that these experienced curriculum developers will show teachers how it is done. The crucial problem is to establish a relationship where they act as consultants, and where their experience serves rather than dictates policy.

There is always likely to be some resistance to change—at any rate a number of individuals may resist it but one can only be positive about proposed changes and aware of possible difficulties. It would be rash to generalise about the nature of innovatory climates; yet it is possible to highlight a number of salient points. The successful organisation of curriculum innovation may depend upon forming a team of volunteers who are willing and able to cooperate with their colleagues. If staff turnover can be kept to a minimum, this will help to provide stability and continuity. During the planning stages of the proposed innovation it is advisable to make careful preparations so that the teachers involved are aware of the conditions in which they will operate and have a clear conception of the task ahead. If it is possible, the timetable should be reorganised to provide planning time for the teachers concerned.

It is essential to create effective means of communication within the group, but it is equally important to keep other members of staff well informed at all stages of the development of any innovation. A 'promotional campaign' may be necessary before any new schemes are put into operation, but this should not be merely an opportunity to inform pupils and parents. An essential factor for success is often the involvement of pupils and parents in the early stages of planning. Those seeking change need above all to remain flexible, and should be adventurous enough to take some risks, encouraging creativity and experimentation within the group. They need to be patient enough to deal with frustration and inevitable setbacks, but patience and persistence usually pay off.

References

EISNER, E. W. (1967) 'Educational Objectives: Help or Hindrance?' *The School Review*, **75**, 3, 250–60.

GOODLAD, J., KLEIN, M. F., *et al.* (1970) *Behind the Classroom Door.* Jones: Worthington, Ohio.

KLEIBARB, H. M. (1970) 'The Tyler rationale'. *The School Review*, **78**, 1, 259–72.

MACDONALD, J. B. (1965) 'Myths about instruction'. *Educational Leadership*, **22**, 613–14.

POPHAM, W. J. (1969) *Objectives and Instruction.* AERA Monograph Series on Curriculum Evaluation, No. 3, 32–52.

SARASON, S. (1971) *The Culture of the School and the Problem of Change.* Allyn and Bacon: Rockleigh, New Jersey.

SMITH, L. and KEITH, P. (1971) *Anatomy of Educational Innovation: an Organizational Analysis of an Elementary School.* Wiley: London.

STENHOUSE, L. (1971) 'Some limitations of the use of objectives in curriculum research and planning'. *Pedagogica Europa*, 73–83.

TAYLOR, P. H. (1972) *Curriculum Planning*. Paper presented at conference, Teacher Involvement in Curriculum Planning, Manchester, 1972. North West Counties P. E. Association.

TYLER, R. W. (1949) *Basic Principles of Curriculum and Instruction.* University of Chicago Press: Chicago.

WISEMAN, S. and PIDGEON, D. (1970) *Curriculum Evaluation.* NFER: London.

CHAPTER FIVE

Integration and the Physical Education Curriculum

Leonard Almond

Integrated studies (or the integrated curriculum) have become the focus for considerable attention as more and more schools change from a curriculum divided by subjects to integrated approaches. Not only are teachers talking about it, they are attempting to put theory into practice. Most of the literature advocating such change appears to assume that the meaning of integrated studies (or integrated curricula) is well understood, and that the only possible problem is to produce recipes for bringing about the state of affairs to which this term refers. However, if one examines proposals for integrated studies courses in CSE Mode III examinations and new courses being developed in the Humanities for middle schools, it becomes apparent that the idea of integration is in fact a cause of much confusion at present: its meaning is not clear and it seems to be susceptible to a variety of interpretations; moreover in educational discussions this variety of interpretations is frequently overlooked. The fact that educational terms are so often subject to misinterpretation is to some extent understandable, but if muddle and confusion are to be avoided we *must* seriously ask the questions: what do they mean by integration? how intelligible is the notion of integration in the curriculum? The purpose of this chapter is to consider the meaning of integration and to explore the position of physical education in relation to the answers to these questions.

Integration

To integrate means to make up a whole from the parts, to combine separate elements. The word presupposes the existence of divisions or separations which may be overcome by integration. The implication behind a desire to integrate is that the traditional curriculum, made up of separate parts, lacks something (the integrationists would claim that the compartmentalised curriculum does not reflect the essential 'wholeness' or 'unity' of experience). However this does not take us very far in a discussion of 'integration' in an educational context where it is often used as an 'approval word'. The desire for approval is strong in educational discourse and the tendency to associate our own activities with the current in-word is difficult to avoid. It is not surprising, therefore, that many teachers have adopted 'integrated' approaches before they have had an opportunity to examine closely the implications either of the term 'integration' or of terms such as 'unity' and 'wholeness'. Nor is it surprising that the schemes of work produced by such teachers often evince a kind of spurious unity without in any way resembling truly integrated curricula.

'Unity' and the differentiation of forms of knowledge

The advocacy for integration in the curriculum is largely a negative movement because it is concerned with rejecting the conventional pattern of a curriculum organised into separate subject compartments. In this conventional pattern the enterprise of achieving complex and varied objectives has been broken down into a series of manageable units called a subject curriculum. This pattern seems to bear some resemblance to the claims made by philosophers for the differentiation of forms of knowledge, or modes of experience. On the basis of conceptual analysis it has been argued that education is concerned with the development of a rational mind. The development of mind involves the progressive differentiation of our experience through the acquisition of concepts which allows us to discriminate between elements of our experience. These concepts, each with its own complex logical structure, form distinctive networks or relationships; therefore, if our experience is capable of being differentiated into a number of distinct forms, or modes, it would appear that the rational way of developing these forms of understanding is to organise the curriculum into units corresponding to these forms. Such an approach is less likely to cause confusion between the various concepts and criteria which reflect the distinctiveness of these forms. The strength of this approach is that it permits systematic attention to be given to the progressive mastery of the most central and fruitful concepts and patterns of reasoning in that particular form. [A detailed account of the structure of knowledge and the justification of subjects has been outlined by Hirst (1965).]

However, the integrationists would counter this by suggesting that even though we must take account of the distinctiveness of various forms of experience, there are interrelationships and connections between these forms, and the curriculum should take account of these connections; the integrationists would claim that the essential 'unity' of experience is reflected in these connections. It does not follow that the best way of developing understanding of our experience is to organise a curriculum into units which reflect the distinctiveness of these forms. There may be many ways of developing this understanding, but this would be an empirical matter of curriculum organisation.

'Integration' in the classroom

In order to consider the meaning of integration and how it is used in the classroom there is a need to isolate examples of so-called integrated work. These examples have been divided into five sections which illustrate different approaches people have taken as a result of their interpretation of the meaning of integration.

(i) Correlation of subjects.
(ii) Project work.
(iii) Interdisciplinary inquiry.

(iv) A proposal for integration.
(v) Integration of teachers.

(*i*) *Correlation of subjects*

In the curriculum there are a number of subjects that have relationships and connections which could be considered as examples of integration; however, examinations of these types do not provide us with much insight into the nature of integration. For example, the solution to certain problems in physics requires a knowledge of mathematics, but the physics teacher cannot hold up experiments if this mathematical knowledge has not been covered. Therefore, he must incorporate this knowledge into his teaching programme to ensure that his pupils have the skill to solve problems, even though such knowledge may be covered at a different stage in mathematics. Cooperation between these two departments may occur, but it is not essential. In the curriculum there are a number of examples of this kind of correlation between subjects.

There are a number of subjects, with structural kinship in concepts and methods, which may be fused on common bases. Subjects like physics, chemistry, and biology for example can be conceived as a single subject, general science, and taught in this way. However, this is very often only for organisational convenience, and within general science the separate components tend to be taught individually. Further examples of this form of integration can be seen in mathematics and English (grammar, literature, composition).

(*ii*) *Project work*

Project work in primary schools provides many examples of so-called integrated work. In one example concerning a project on 'water', a young and relatively inexperienced teacher was able to organise a complete scheme of activities in which pupils were able to investigate problems in science, mathematics and geography. They were to relate this work to creative writing, poetry and painting. This was supplemented by listening to music about the sea which was supposed to stir their imagination and stimulate them to find different stories and songs about the sea (incidentally we ill-prepare pupils to develop musical skills and a feeling for music if we imply that they should relate musical experience to everything else). Valuable swimming time was devoted to exploring and experimenting with water so that the pupils could express their feelings and thoughts at the time of the experience. The pupils were also expected to relate this experience to their work in science and mathematics, though no attempt was made to link what was done in the water with activities that illustrated similar principles.

In the secondary school one constantly hears of similar ideas being used involving themes such as 'communication'. If this were the theme, the English specialist might give a lead lesson followed by a talk on literature as a means of communication. The history teacher might then organise activities around a topic such as the development of trans-port; and the RE teacher might discuss the importance of prayer in a relationship with God. Where is the integration of the curriculum in an organisation of this sort? How is the pupil to unify such divergent ideas?

I have no quarrel with project work—on 'water' or 'com-munication'—that links experiences or subjects and that has some regard to the concepts, principles, or skills a pupil could develop during this process. But to achieve this level of integration teachers would need some organising principle that they might use in order to link different experiences which would allow the pupil to establish relationships, see connections, and build new concepts. No doubt the experi-ence that the teachers provided in my examples had a meaning within a wider context, but it seems doubtful that their pupils would be able to see this meaning. Far too many projects artificially contrive to establish tenuous links be-tween experiences which really have very little in common other than their rather general title.

(iii) Interdisciplinary inquiry

Many middle-school courses in the Humanities appear to have taken up the theme of 'Man' as the focus point for integrated projects. The stimulus for this approach may have come from a number of Schools Council publications and from the development of School Broadcasts which use 'Man' as the basis for integrated-studies programmes. Schools Council Working Paper No. 2 suggests that a 'sound basis for development is the study of Man' (p. 12). This is supported both by Working Paper No. 11 which suggests that a curriculum about man 'may mean less emphasis on the barriers between traditional subjects and more upon their interrelationships' (p. 1), and by Working Paper No. 22 which informs us that ' "Man and his environment" represents an integration of disciplines' (p. 45). It is likely that statements of this kind have supported moves by teachers away from separate subjects and the adoption of so-called new areas of study which are often considered to be more relevant to the pupil.

But, can we consider these to be new areas of inquiry with their own particular conceptual structure and distinctive concepts, or do they represent a selective principle by which relevant material is chosen? This is an important point that needs to be stressed because integration incorporates the idea of unity between different forms of knowledge and understanding, whereas what is intended could be simply the application of disciplines, in their diverse forms, to a particular range of questions. In the latter case this would be interdisciplinary inquiry rather than an integrated inquiry. This distinction between integration and interdisciplinary inquiry is important because it has different implications for how teachers plan their courses and for the kinds of questions that need to be explored if pupils are to develop understanding in the Humanities.

We do not wish to ask new questions about 'Man' as an area of study, but there is a need to decide which questions about 'Man' will best develop understanding in terms both of the pupils' learning process and of the organisation of subject matter. The idea of integration incorporates a notion of unity between different forms of knowledge, implying a conceptual unity in our thinking, whereas interdisciplinary inquiry refers to the use of more than one discipline, or subject, in pursuing a particular inquiry.

(iv) A proposal for integration

It has been argued by Entwistle (1970) that integrated studies is a poor instrument for acquiring disciplined knowledge and skill, and he suggests that the value of the integrated approach lies in the experience it can provide in teaching pupils to approach social problems from a number of different angles. Such problems often fall outside or across distinctive disciplines. Therefore, by integrating certain aspects of the curriculum around social or moral problems we encourage children to examine experience from as many relevant viewpoints as possible in order that they can resist prejudiced conclusions and opinions. One project which could be said to incorporate this proposal is the Schools Council Humanities Project where the principle of integration adopted is the relevance of empirical inquiries to the understanding of controversial moral, social and political issues.

The Humanities Curriculum Project aims to encourage pupils to develop understanding of a plurality of values and attitudes which influence people's actions in life situations. In order to explore, understand and critically evaluate the complexity of human acts, situations and the controversial value-issues they pose, a procedure has been developed which enables the teacher's behaviour to facilitate these aims. During the exploration of different value systems the teacher has a duty to protect minority opinion and pupil autonomy, expose divergent views and maintain critical standards, and at the same time allow pupils autonomy and freedom to choose their own commitments.

Elliott (1972) in a description of this project explains how the materials of this course are used:

> He may help them to explore differing value-systems in the context of discussions, and to facilitate this he may place before them materials embodying a variety of 'value-systems', 'world-views', or 'normative conceptions of life'. Poetry, painting, literature, films, letters, diaries, etc. can all be of help here. An understanding of the values and

attitudes embodied in these, demands close attention to the content of the materials, and since individuals are prone to be selective in their interpretations (so that they do not conflict with or threaten their own values) the teacher will encourage a diversity of interpretations in the hope that the fullest understanding is developed through group discussion.

(v) *Integration of teachers*

A concern for integration of subjects is also associated with the integration of personnel and the removal of constant breaks in the timetable. It is often argued that integration of subjects may contribute towards a more intelligent approach to learning because it allows a more flexible grouping of pupils, removes the barrier of recurrent breaks and involves teachers in the cooperative enterprise of team teaching. However, these so-called advantages are not necessarily the by-products of the integration of subjects. Because pupils are involved in individualised patterns of work with access to a number of teachers and they are unhindered by artificial breaks, there is no reason to suggest that they are involved in the integration of subjects. In fact PE teachers have employed team teaching for many years without any integration of subjects.

However, team teaching itself is a form of integration and there is a sense in which it is required by all the staff of a school because they need to cooperate with one another in the joint enterprise of educating their pupils. As this idealistic conception bears little resemblance to reality, we must approach the idea of team teaching from a different point of view. The advocates of team teaching claim that, by establishing a team which is collectively responsible for a large group of pupils, a wider range of teaching skills and competences is made available and that this allows a more flexible form of organisation. Within this organisation there is more opportunity to plan individual and collaborative modes of learning with access to a wide range of resources (the use of a centralised resource area); it also enables pupils to have more access to adult figures who have different skills and competences. In addition it greatly facilitates the introduction of new or inexperienced teachers into a particular teaching situation because they can take on a full teaching-load gradually. The teachers can also learn from seeing and hearing their own colleagues.

The threat of standardisation

A word of caution has been expressed over the trend to integrate curricula. Musgrove (1973) has suggested that the move away from subject departments and the centralisation of power and authority in a few large faculties will produce standardisation, servility and lack of vitality. If this thesis is correct, and there is every indication that this can happen, the movement for curriculum development must rethink and re-examine its own aims or objectives and strategies for innovation. Musgrove argues for schools that possess loose confederations of subject departments which accentuate diversity and distinctions in the curriculum. He believes that subject pluralism, flexibility and decentralisation of power in a school will promote change rather than prevent it.

However, an essential component in this sort of organisation will be coordination and cooperation between staff. It will be necessary for individual staff and subject specialists to come together to decide the curriculum and keep it under constant review as a result of evaluation and debate. In this sort of organisation there will be a need for responsibility, integrity, a willingness to participate and courage in the face of evaluation.

One can have every sympathy for Musgrove's thesis because it is one in which parents, pupils and staff have the opportunity to plan curricula which contain genuine and meaningful choices. Pupils should be able to make choices, be responsible for their choice, and face the possible consequences. Where there is plurality and diversity in lifestyles there is a need for people to make responsible choices. The word of caution expressed by Musgrove is an indication that single subjects and integrated projects are not curricular alternatives. Their educational functions are complementary rather than mutually exclusive: within a person's education

there should be opportunity for widely different mo
learning.

Integration in physical education

Several subjects, and physical education is no exception
here, have been accused on occasions of jumping on the
bandwagon of the latest educational fad or trying to apply a
new theory without question to the activities that teachers
organise. It would appear that this tendency could become a
real danger for physical education teachers when their colleagues are urged to integrate. Most teachers appear to
accept that integration is good but few have made a real
attempt to understand its implications or even its meaning.

The danger seems to lie in an implicit belief in integration—a belief which is often followed either by a search
for ways in which the physical education programme can be
given some semblance of integration, or by a desire to
combine with other subjects suggesting certain features that
illustrate a conception of integration. These products are
commended without question simply because they have been
given the title, 'Integrated'. In order to expose this danger it
seems necessary to examine several types of activity in a
physical education programme which demonstrate different
conceptions of integration. The intention is not to make
general assertions about these conceptions of integration,
but to examine the basis on which they are made.

Successful integration

In school A, the physical education programme has been
organised so that large groups of pupils under the direction
of a number of specialist teachers are allowed to select and
make a commitment to one particular activity for a given
period of time; this is followed by the opportunity to make a
further selection at a later date. It is claimed that the value of
this form of organisation is that it enables the teaching and

pos. school timetable setup to bad

to advantageous P.E. in prim. school

coaching to be conducted by specialists with knowledge, skill and insight relating to a particular activity. This kind of specialist coaching, it is claimed, may promote better learning and involvement for the pupils.

On certain afternoons each week the head of the physical education department has cooperated with the music, drama and craft departments to create large blocks of time in which pupils elect for one activity covering a set period of time. At the end of this period the pupils make a further choice in a different subject. This opportunity enables both pupils and teachers to get away from school in order to tackle activities like climbing and sailing that require specialist facilities. Travelling time is less of a problem and the pupils benefit by getting away from the school situation.

In addition to cooperating with other departments for organisational convenience, the head of the department has also forged a number of links with the craft and environmental studies departments. As a result of an interest in canoe building, several pupils have made their own canoes using the opportunity provided by the craft department for pupils to develop their own projects. This interest has been extended so that the PE department has been able to equip their outdoor pursuits section with a number of canoes.

The environmental studies department has undertaken a number of field trips which have enabled pupils to become involved in activities that demonstrate the ideas learnt in the classroom, and which have given them the opportunity to develop skills that cannot be achieved in a classroom situation. Many of these trips involve camping; therefore the expertise of the PE department has been used to prepare adequately for these excursions. This link with the PE department has resulted in other outdoor pursuits (canoeing for example) being added to the programme of the field trips. In this way the two departments have come together to plan joint field trips which have enabled pupils to experience activities that cannot be undertaken in the school environment. The scope of the two departments has widened, and, in addition, it has been possible to reinforce the learning of certain skills in a competitive situation, for example the learning of navigation skills through orienteering. In this way both departments have a unique opportunity to share concepts and skills.

School A provides non-controversial examples of integration—between subjects, teachers and departments—and one would expect most physical education teachers to be well aware of the potential of such cooperation. These examples are, in fact, no more than good management. However, it is important to point out that they *are* forms of integration and that physical education *is* involved with integration—of a non-controversial nature. However, physical education is also involved with aspects of so called 'integration' which constitute a real danger to the subject.

Unsuccessful 'integration'

School B has no distinguishable timetable and the curriculum is centred round projects rather than subjects. Themes and topical interests initiate and stimulate the development of project work. For one project—on the Olympic Games—it was possible to associate a number of traditional subjects like science, mathematics, geography, history and poetry with the type of work that the teacher thought would be appropriate for an examination of this theme. Well before the event, work cards were carefully planned and linked with numerous activities that would involve the pupils in collecting and finding out information. A variety of sporting activities were planned to involve all the pupils in striving for gold, silver and bronze medals in a mini-Olympics. At the completion of this project the pupils started a new one on 'pilots and flying'.

The staff at school B are concerned for all aspects of their pupils' education; therefore they have read the publication, *Movement* (DES, 1972) and they have adopted the suggestion:

> ... there might be special value in combining subjects such as literature, drama, music and science that have a natural link with some aspects of physical education ... (p. 22)

Consequently they have sought ways in which PE can illustrate particular concepts in science and mathematics, and vice versa. Movement lessons have been used to produce a dance-drama production based on Hallowe'en. Some of the creative writing and poetry related to this dance-drama revealed a vocabulary of movement which had obviously been used in movement lessons. Every opportunity has been sought to relate concepts in movement to other areas of work where there may be a relationship.

School B has designed an inquiry-based curriculum in which one of the main criteria for selecting content is topical interest. All the planned activities serve inquiry-based learning; therefore contributions from different 'traditional' subjects would only be selected if they were able to illuminate the topic or chosen theme. One of the interesting things about this approach is the way in which the curriculum often reflects adult assumptions about what pupils ought to be interested in. Pupils may well be interested in the Olympic Games for example, but teachers should not assume that pupils will only learn when they are involved in topics of obvious immediate appeal: the achievement of personal satisfaction is but one objective that a school is concerned with in inquiry-based learning; it should not be the overriding concern. Surely, the teacher is also concerned with creating new interests!

It is at this point that questions arise about the selection of physical education activities that may be included in projects. There seem to be three main points that ought to be made about this: they concern

  (i) the short-term project,
  (ii) the 'natural links' between literature, science and physical education, and
  (iii) the spiral curriculum.

(i) The short-term project

In projects of this type which only last a short period, physical education takes on a casual image because it is seen merely as relaxation from more demanding intellectual activities. Little opportunity is provided to tackle an activity in any depth. In this situation the mini-Olympics organised by school B hardly reflects the culmination of dedicated work, determination and skill exemplified in the Olympic competitor.

A mini-Olympics reflecting activities from a balanced and varied programme carried out over a longer period of time would be a far more valuable exercise. However, many teachers involved in short-term projects appear to think that the real objectives of physical education may be disregarded: pupils are sometimes introduced to an entirely new activity which is dropped after a short time—when the project is over; any ability or interest is capitalised upon for the moment; and little opportunity is provided for any further development or follow up. In situations of this type there are few educational opportunities of any value, because as far as physical education is concerned the experience is only of a transient nature.

(ii) The 'natural links' between literature, science and physical education

What are these 'natural links'? There may be some connections between work in science and the pupil's work in movement, but it does not follow that movement work should have to illustrate scientific concepts or that science should have to illustrate concepts in movement. However, in science lessons there is nothing wrong in illustrating a point by reference to movement education, or even planning activities in which pupils perform movements that demonstrate certain principles. This enactive mode of representation (Bruner, 1966) is a powerful medium for learning and it deserves further consideration in education. Similarly in movement lessons, by all means point out scientific or mathematical principles that appear to be relevant or that provide the pupils with an organising idea. But when a project is being organised it is important to ask whether movement work will be used principally to illustrate concepts from other areas of work or whether the objectives of movement education should dictate the activities of movement lessons.

In other words, should the movement lesson have an 'instrumental' role or an 'intrinsic' role. When planning a project that calls for integration or reference to 'natural links' between subjects, there is always the danger of allocating an instrumental role to movement education. The PE teacher should resist this threat to his subject: even though one can see possibilities for exemplifying other objectives in a movement lesson, they should not dominate procedures in the teaching of movement; moreover the 'natural links' between physical education and other subjects (science, maths, literature) should be treated as possible 'spin-offs' of a movement lesson and not as its *raison d'être*.

The 'natural links' between literature and physical education are difficult to envisage because what the authors of *Movement* (DES, 1972, p. 22) appear to mean by 'natural links' in this context is that physical education can stir the imagination or create ideas that can be developed in creative writing or poetry. In this sense the vocabulary must be the 'natural link', or rather the only connection. We must not delude ourselves that 'natural links' of this nature are justifiable reasons for integration, or even examples of integration.

(iii) The spiral curriculum

When projects are selected there seems to be little or no connection between projects undertaken last week, the current project and the one for next week; consequently there is very little continuity in the pupils' education, very little connection between the concepts and skills that the pupils develop during one week and those they develop the next week. This seems to suggest a lack of integration. Surely, integrating knowledge and experience should involve the relating of current experience with our past experience, and a recasting of this knowledge in the development of new concepts. The concept of a spiral curriculum, which is often quoted by integrationists advocating project work, involves just this type of activity. Yet it is very apparent that project work in many schools is not related in this sense. The integrationists may have adopted Whitehead's prescription, 'let the main ideas which are introduced into a child's education be few and important, and let them be thrown into every combination possible' (Whitehead, 1955, p. 3), but they have ignored his notion of a cyclical process of learning. In this process (which is very similar to Bruner's concept of the spiral curriculum) what is learned now, grows out of earlier learning. Learning involves both horizontal and vertical relationships between ideas, a point which project work often seems to ignore. An examination of projects undertaken by pupils over a whole term often reveals a complete disregard for this notion; yet the teachers have advocated an integrated curriculum.

If there are fundamental concepts in movement education that need to be developed—taking into account that what is learned grows out of earlier learning—then teachers need to be aware of the dangers of allowing projects to dominate their selection of movement work. It may be possible to outline a course of movement education in which experienced teachers can utilise projects and topical interests as motivations and which enriches work done in other areas of the curriculum. But PE teachers must not allow project work to detract from what is done in movement lessons or allow the project approach to turn the movement lesson into a series of non-sequential events subserving the objectives of literature or science education.

Integration or inter-disciplinary inquiry

In any discussion about integration, the central concern seems to be the elimination of subject barriers, individual disciplines and the organizational framework that compartmentalises the curriculum. The reason for this concern is the failure of the compartmentalised curriculum to reveal the complex interrelationships between the different sorts of knowledge and to show how certain concepts transcend the artificial barriers that divide subjects. Because of this, proposals are made for the integration of certain subjects into new organisations that will examine common concepts and ideas: in the Humanities, for example, pupils are encouraged to study themes like 'Man', and to examine controversial moral and social issues like 'conflict'.

However, are these new organisations merely attempts to demonstrate interrelationships and connections between concepts, or are they new distinctive forms of study with a new structure of thought? It seems quite clear from reading many of these proposals that what teachers are trying to do is merely to demonstrate interrelationships and connections, and to show how developments in one discipline affect developments in another, rather than to produce a new area of study; therefore when they speak of integration of subjects, they are really referring to inter-disciplinary inquiry.

Different level of integration

It is difficult to see how it would be possible to develop understanding of concepts like 'conflict' and 'power' without the cooperation of different subjects. But physical education is hardly concerned with cooperation on this level because the subject is not involved with complex interrelationships between different forms of knowledge or with the need for these connections to be made explicit. The place of physical education in the curriculum does not depend upon its epistemological status; therefore any possible connections and relationships with other subjects are on an entirely different level. This distinction is important because physical educationists who advocate integration with other subjects seem to assume that they are on the same level. It is this distinction which is often forgotten when movement work is linked with the development of scientific and mathematical concepts in the hope that this cooperation will aid such development, and create more insight into the pupil's movement work. In this interpretation there seems to be confusion about the purpose of movement work, and confusion between the 'means' and the 'ends' of an activity; in this case movement work becomes the means for achieving some end outside of the activity itself. The criteria for selecting movement activities are based on how well these activities will develop scientific and mathematical concepts;

so there is a move away from the intrinsic value of movement work in a pupil's development, to one where it has merely an instrumental role in which movement work could be discarded if it failed to develop appropriate concepts. Thus, teachers must be clear about the purpose of movement work and its place in the curriculum, because only then can they consider the level at which they are trying to integrate.

It is at this point that one must consider three possible levels at which integration of subjects can operate:

(a) The bringing together of different forms of knowledge to promote understanding of concepts (like 'conflict') which are shared by these disciplines; this is inter-disciplinary inquiry.
(b) The bringing together of subjects to develop understanding of concepts in one subject area because certain activities in another can help to promote this understanding. In this case certain scientific concepts can be demonstrated by reference to movement work, and there can be no objection to this procedure so long as the 'natural links' are considered to be latent spin-offs rather than the central point of the activity. This does not represent integration of subjects where epistemological questions about the structure of knowledge and the correlation of interconnecting concepts are essential.
(c) The bringing together of subjects because the skills of one subject are useful to another. Thus, the physical education department may cooperate with the home economics department in the preparation of menus for a camping expedition, or with the craft department in the building of canoes; but this is not, of course, inter-disciplinary inquiry.

However, although there may appear to be three levels at which one can consider integration of subjects in relation to physical education in schools, in fact PE, as a discipline, cannot be part of an inter-disciplinary inquiry. Pupils studying 'conflict' may examine this concept in the context of a football match where different varieties of 'conflict' may occur; but in this inter-disciplinary inquiry the questions that one would be asking could be historical, sociological and psychological, and sport would be merely the content for the study, just like a study of conflict in Northern Ireland would be. Thus, physical education is not one of the disciplines brought together for the purpose of the inquiry; it is merely the content of the inquiry.

In these forms of inquiry—where pupils are encouraged to study society, social problems and social situations—topics such as 'sporting attitudes', 'leisure', 'mass media' and 'sport' are obviously appropriate areas of inquiry because they provide opportunities for studying human actions and the value-issues they pose. If issues of this nature are being investigated and discussed in class, there is every possibility that pupils' attitudes to physical education will be fundamentally altered. In the same way, an inter-disciplinary inquiry about 'Man' in a Humanities course can include the notion of 'sporting man'; this may provide insight into the nature of 'Man', and could influence the pupils' thinking about sport and its influence on people's lives. However, we must not consider that the inclusion of these ideas in the curriculum calls for the integration of physical education with those disciplines used in an inquiry. Certain areas of sport (which are part of physical education) can be incorporated into the curriculum without the involvement of physical education as a subject; there is no necessity to consider its inclusion as a subject as being essential to the development of understanding in these areas. On the other hand, there is no reason why the physical education teacher cannot be used as a consultant to advise other teachers about the use of sport for the content of an inquiry.

So far, this paper has been concerned with examining various conceptions of the integration of subjects in the curriculum, and the way this has influenced physical education. In examining these conceptions it has been necessary to point out certain dangers that have arisen as a result of implementing integrated curricula. It is relatively easy to point out dangers and express criticism of practical situations, but this criticism has been made because it raises a fundamental point, among others, about how teachers decide their curricula. In making proposals for integrated curricula, how often do teachers consider whether their new offerings are better than those which they have replaced? In order to answer a question of this nature, it seems essential for schools to have the machinery for making such considerations, because without it they cannot seriously entertain any notion of integration and cooperation between subjects.

An operational model of integrated curriculum planning

In the construction of any curriculum, political conflict is generated by the existence of competing values concerning what should be taught in a school. An agency of some sort should be responsible for allocating these competing values in some way, even though this will mean that some interests will win and others lose on particular curriculum issues. At the present moment there is no rational yardstick for the selection of priorities among these values, and there is no agency other than a head-teacher for making such considerations. But, if the curriculum is an important factor in the education of pupils, there does appear to be a necessity for integration among *teachers* to consider *jointly* the process of curriculum policy-making. Therefore, before there can be any talk of integration of subjects, there is a more urgent need for teachers to come together to plan curricula (at this stage this paper is not concerned with the justification of involving parents and pupils in integration; this is a much broader issue that is worthy of further debate). The cooperation and coordination of teachers is essential if they are to implement the objectives of the school, because if there is no integration of purpose, it is difficult to see how teachers can seriously make proposals for any form of integration that is going to have a meaning.

Lawton (1969) in *The Idea of the Integrated Curriculum* suggested a possible operational model of integrated curriculum planning for a school. In his model there are three levels of organisation: the first is concerned with the formation of a group responsible for planning the whole curriculum of the school; the second is concerned with intra-disciplinary integration to ensure maximum cooperation and coordination of teachers within a particular subject department; the third level is inter-disciplinary integration where there is cooperation and coordination between departments. At first glance this would appear to be a rather obvious prescription and one that many schools would adopt; yet the plain truth is that there are very few schools which operate this kind of system. In most schools there simply does not seem to be a coherent system of organisation bringing *all* teachers together in the curriculum-planning process.

However, Lawton's prescription requires careful examination because the setting up of committees and the holding of numerous meetings may not be the complete answer to the need for a more rational approach to curricula construction. This is because the rationality associated with curriculum planning is not the same as scientific or legal rationality. Taylor (1972) argues this point by suggesting that:

> It is more like political rationality and the rationality of diplomacy. In the end it is a form of social rationality, the grounds for which are neither provable nor disprovable; but they are no more than the basis of evidence on which people are willing to accept that something is desirable.

This may be the case, but in curriculum policy-making the final choices among competing claims may depend upon the relative power of particular groups or subject departments rather than the cogency of their arguments in putting forward proposals. This highlights the necessity for teachers to commit themselves to an active involvement in policy-making, to present justifiable claims which are free from subject-bias, to be aware of the basis for other people's claims, and as far as possible to ensure that decisions are made which take into account all relevant interests.

Because 'political rationality' prevails in the staffroom, physical education departments have a tendency to keep themselves as a separate component in the school, with very little chance of exerting any influence in the area of curriculum policy-making. However, if schools are concerned with moral education for example, physical education departments ought to be aware of the possibilities for such development within the context of teaching their subject, and they should communicate this information to the policy-makers. Moreover, schools cannot claim to have a real concern for moral education unless they have considered how each department can contribute to this development.

Physical education may be pursuing objectives which are specific to the subject, but there is no reason why it should not also be aware of possible latent objectives like moral education which are considered to be valuable in the general education of the pupil. In fact, physical education seems to offer many opportunities for latent objectives which are part of the general objectives of the school; and so long as teachers are aware which are latent objectives and they are not allowed to dominate procedures in the teaching of physical education, there is no reason why they cannot be incorporated into the contribution made by physical education to the education of the pupil.

Physical education departments cannot continue to retain a separate identity: they should concern themselves with the whole curriculum as well as their own subject. They should be aware of the basis of claims made by other subjects, and it may be that they should be prepared to teach other subjects as well as their own specialism. By teaching other subsubjects one does become more aware of the value and limitations of one's own specialist knowledge and skill, in addition to gaining insight into what the curriculum can offer a pupil. Consequently, the integration of teachers and the establishment of some body or agency for formulating the curriculum could mean that physical education departments will have more opportunity to become involved in curriculum decisions that will affect the whole school, rather than be affected by decisions that tend to be made without their involvement.

References

BRUNER, J. S. (1966) *Toward a Theory of Instruction.* Norton: New York.

DEPARTMENT OF EDUCATION AND SCIENCE. (1972) *Movement: physical education in the primary years.* HMSO: London.

ELLIOTT, J. (1972) 'The integration of the curriculum' in BIRNIE, I. H. (ed.) *Religious Education in Integrated Studies.* SCM Press: London.

ENTWHISTLE, H. (1970) *Child-centred Education.* Methuen: London.

HIRST, P. H. (1965) 'Liberal education and the nature of knowledge' in ARCHAMBAULT, R. D. (ed.) *Philosophical Analysis and Education.* Routledge and Kegan Paul: London.

LAWTON, D. (1969) *The Idea of an Integrated Curriculum*, University of London Institute of Education Bulletin No. 19.

MUSGROVE, F. (1973) 'Power and the Integrated Curriculum'. *Journal of Curriculum Studies*, **5**, 1.

TAYLOR, P. H. (1972) *Curriculum Planning.* Paper presented at conference, Teacher Involvement in Curriculum Planning, Manchester, 1972. North West Counties PE Association.

WHITEHEAD, A. N. (1955) *The Aims of Education.* Williams & Norgate: London.

CHAPTER SIX

Curriculum Development in Practice

Alan Gibbon

It was tempting, in writing this chapter, to range far and wide, and describe programmes and innovations which, though exciting, were not familiar to the writer. However, in visits to schools, it was found that what teachers said they were doing and even what was reported by independent observers, rarely bore any resemblance to what was actually going on. This confirmed my suspicion that many innovations in physical education, and presumably elsewhere in the curriculum, exist at an ideological rather than substantive level and I decided, as far as possible, to describe programmes and innovations of which I had first-hand knowledge.

This clearly limits the scope of the chapter and even, perhaps, gives it a rather haphazard flavour but it does, at least, ensure that it is the realities of curriculum development that are considered—'applied' curriculum development hammered out in the school situation and which pays only token respect, if any, to laboratory based 'pure' forms hawked about by 'curriculum mongers' in institutes of higher education and even by Schools Council Curriculum Project teams.

For the purposes of this chapter a definition of the curriculum is used which embraces what are sometimes called 'curricular' and 'extra-curricular' activities. The definition is: 'All activities deliberately planned and guided by the school or local education authority to bring about changes in the pupils'.

Implicit in such a definition is the assumption that activities of all kinds, from school clubs to inter-house and inter-school competitions, and (in the context of this chapter) local authority special-ability classes, which normally take place outside school hours, should be integral parts of the overall physical education programme of an education authority and of the schools within it. Such 'extra-curricular' activities should be a reflection and an extension of the interest stimulated in the gymnasium or on the playing-field during 'curriculum' time rather than, as they are so often, the products of a 'creaming process by which large numbers of children have been rejected' (McNab, 1970).

Peter McIntosh (Chapter 1) has traced the development of the physical education curriculum from its games-dominated era in the public schools of the nineteenth century to the 'variegated and bewildering pattern of activities' offered by many secondary schools today. In this chapter I will first describe, and briefly comment on, the physical education programme of a secondary school which is probably now fairly typical of the programmes offered by secondary schools in this country, certainly those of a comprehensive type. This will, it is hoped, act as a kind of touchstone for the examination of various curriculum innovations which have been attempted recently and which seem to merit some attention.

Physical education—programme of a large comprehensive school

The physical education department of this school has produced a printed syllabus which clearly states their aims and which also acts as a guide to the running of the physical education programme for any new members of staff.

The opening statement of the introduction sums up the basic philosophy of the department. 'The comprehensive nature of the school must be remembered when organising the physical education programme. Not all children are equally endowed with the physical skills needed for sporting activities, nor are they equally interested in traditional physical activities. We must cater for all interests and build upon them.' Their aims are formed with the above statement in mind:

(a) to promote the normal growth and development of each pupil according to his own capacity;
(b) to provide each pupil with a wide range of movement in order that his vocabulary of movement is not restricted;
(c) to encourage and develop skill in chosen specialised forms of movement;
(d) to develop awareness of others, cooperation with others and individual determination;
(e) to arouse in the pupils a desire to continue active participation in physical activities after leaving school.

The compilers of this syllabus believe that all the activities in any physical education programme have a common factor: 'movement'. Movement is then broken down into four parts, each needing to be developed within the programme:

(a) *movement exploration* (educational gymnastics—to give efficient use of the body and knowledge of movement);
(b) *teaching of special skills of movement* (sports of all kinds);
(c) *creative expression through movement* (educational dance and dance drama);
(d) *efficient movement through a strong healthy body* (this aspect should be covered by the work of the whole programme).

These four aspects of movement provide the basis of the work of the department and determine the content of the basic course of educational gymnastics, dance, games of all types and basic fitness. In the first, second and third years all pupils have two 35-minute periods in the gymnasium and one double-period of games per week. Boys, for example, follow courses of educational gymnastics, dance, basic skills, rugby, soccer and hockey and athletics. All the pupils who cannot swim are required to attend the baths for swimming instruction.

In the fourth and fifth years all pupils have one 35-minute period in the gymnasium and a double-period of games per week. They have a choice of activities such as trampolining, basketball, strength contests, volley-ball, gymnastics, judo and as wide a choice of games activities as possible. The sixth year may opt to do games with the fifth year.

The basic skills course was initiated because it was felt that many pupils were lacking basic games skills upon entry to the secondary school. During this course the basic skills of catching, throwing, hitting, etc., are intensively practised.

There is evidence here of a department that has formulated its aims fairly carefully and developed a programme which has some hope of achieving some of them at least. The programme also, in its language and design, illustrates how three post-war innovations have been assimilated into the modern physical education curriculum:

(a) an acceptance of the language of movement education and a differentiation within it of two quite separate activities—educational gymnastics and educational dance;

(b) the acceptance of dance into the programme for boys, though it would be wrong to claim that this is widespread;

(c) the introduction of optional activities, particularly for older pupils.

In essence, the programme follows what might be called a 'funnel' (Figure 6.1) pattern in that it starts with a number of basic courses, with no choice for pupils, which lasts for three years and then broadens out into first limited and then free options, chosen from a large number of activities.

Schools following such a programme will vary as to both the numbers and kinds of basic courses they provide in the lower school and the range of options they offer in the upper school. Some will have a short stem to the funnel, offering limited options as early as the third year, while others will have a longer stem to the funnel, delaying options until the fifth and sixth years. Many schools, particularly selective schools, do, still, of course, follow a traditional programme of gymnastics and major games with no options at any stage.

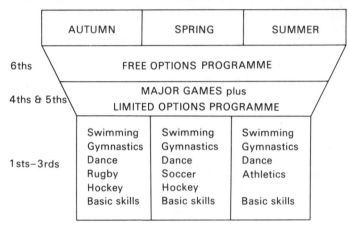

Figure 6.1   'Funnel' programme

It is not suggested that one kind of programme is better than another. So much still depends on the individual circumstances of schools in terms of staff, facilities, time, money and, not least, tradition. The 'funnel' type of programme just described was primarily developed in order to offer a range of activities to older pupils who had not achieved a level of success in the compulsory basic course, and which might encourage them to pursue one activity at least in the upper school and even in post-school life. It was hoped that as more activities, on an optional basis, were made available, the number of reluctant performers, even non-participants, would decrease if not disappear. This appears to have been an optimistic assessment. There may be all sorts of reasons for this, but one seems to be worth considering.

Perhaps many of the activities are offered too late. It is, presumably, just as difficult, or easy, to learn squash or golf as it is rugby or hockey. I know of no evidence that suggests otherwise, and by the time pupils 'discover' squash or golf in the optional programme in the upper school it may be too late to give them enough time at the activity to enable them to reach a reasonable level of skill, a level of skill that will give them the confidence to join a club when they leave school; this is almost certainly crucial to post-school participation and an area worthy of further research.

Perhaps the whole concept of options for older pupils only, after a basic compulsory course in the lower school, is totally misguided. One teacher expresses his misgivings about this most succinctly in an article which bears closer examination.

> No one would think of teaching mathematics, English or science and then *select* the failures in these subjects to try and find some comfort in history or French ... the system is doomed to failure from the beginning because of heads of departments using options as a means of cleaning up their major sports groups. Horse-riding becomes a gilt-edged rubbish tip for the sick, the lame and the lazy (Chapman, 1972).

This raises all sorts of questions about what we should include in the physical education programme and at what age various activities should be introduced; but alas, questions I cannot tackle within the limits of this chapter—they are touched upon in other chapters.

Although the approach to curriculum planning attempted by the staff of this comprehensive school will not satisfy everyone, particularly, perhaps, those who believe that a behavioural objective approach is both universally applicable and desirable, it is the result of much careful thought and teamwork. And it does seem to work, in this school at least, if only in terms of the whole-hearted involvement of all the staff and the great majority of pupils, and the attainment of a reasonable level of skill by a large proportion of the pupils.

School physical education and the outside world

The raising of the school-leaving age in England and Wales to sixteen in 1973 has stimulated some interesting innovations principally designed to help young people to use their leisure time purposefully when they leave school.

One school has developed a course that is designed to cover one day per week for one school year; pupils are also expected to give some of their own time as part of the course.

The aims are to provide a course of study that will give

(a) a greater understanding of leisure;
(b) a confidence to use this understanding in the practical situation;
(c) practical experience of leisure activities.

The course includes talks by experts on such topics as, the function of a Borough Recreation Department, compiling a questionnaire, visual display techniques, joining a Youth Club or Evening Institute, sports reporting, financing leisure, the formation and running of a club, active holidays, medical aspects of leisure activities, factors affecting health and fitness, therapeutic value of leisure, and sports injuries. A visit is planned to a multi-sports complex and, near the end of the course, all students are taken to the country for a week to live together under canvas and to learn basic camping and the use of the countryside.

Throughout the course the students have the task of studying the facilities for sport and recreation in the immediate area of their school, as well as joining a club of their own choice and an evening class to learn a new activity. This course differs from many developing as a result of the raising of the school leaving age (ROSLA) in that the students are encouraged to make personal contact with the local sports facilities instead of having all the contacts made for them. The forging of links between schools and clubs, youth service and adult education would appear to be an essential part of the physical education of older pupils, for such links provide pupils with an avenue to post-school physical recreation and help them to develop an awareness of adult-status—an awareness that is so vital to their self-esteem.

In another school the physical education department have looked at this problem of designing a course to suit the older pupils and have instituted what they call a 'Culture Course'.

The staff had long felt that some aspects of the subject could not be covered adequately in the time allowed and indeed that some aspects had to be ignored altogether. It was felt that some of these aspects could be usefully combined together to form a course that would be both interesting and of value to the fourth-year pupil and could well help to avert any fading of interest in the subject that often takes place at this age.

Besides covering aspects not fully exploited in the normal scheme of work, it was felt that a scheme of this nature should extend and fulfil the interests of those pupils who in their earlier school life had shown a natural aptitude for the subject. These aims led them to design a course involving three sections:

(a) outdoor pursuits to cover country code, map reading and orienteering, camping, hiking and route planning, basic first aid and the effects of exposure;
(b) swimming to cover ASA Silver Survival Award, resuscitation, life saving and water safety;
(c) theory block to cover history and hygiene, practical options in research, statistics, etc.

In addition to this work, there are talks and discussions led by outside speakers on topics of interest such as smoking, venereal disease, the work of the Sports Council, family planning, etc. The pupils are expected to attend camps organised by the school. The course is designed to cover a period of one year working on two 35-minute periods per week with extra time for visits.

Both the courses described are examples of curriculum development that has come as a result of the raising of the school leaving age. The first course places a great amount of importance on preparing the pupils for the time when they leave school, and it gives them every encouragement to continue with active participation in physical activity when they do leave. The second includes a large amount of physical work as part of the course, and in so doing probably

gears it to the pupils who enjoy physical activity and who
have had a certain amount of success in previous years.

Two questions arise here; first whether these are the
pupils who are most in need of such a course and, second
and perhaps more fundamental, whether it is right to isolate
a ROSLA group and plan special courses for it. I will return
to this point later in discussing a General Studies course for
sixth formers.

Outdoor education

In recent years there has been a move to take education
away from the traditional confines of the school and into the
world beyond, whether it be the immediate surrounding
vicinity of the school or much further afield. This movement
has, in the first place, been rather haphazard, with each
subject going its own way in search of its own particular
specialisation. In some areas, however, this movement has
been coordinated in order that outdoor education can be a
part of the whole school-curriculum, with many subjects
contributing their own specialisms so that students gain as
much as possible from expeditions away from their school.

In Canada, money was provided for a detailed study to be
undertaken to look into what was going on in this field, and
to recommend how it should be developed. The report shows
that many subjects can profitably use outdoor education
programmes to support the work done in the classroom. A
few examples are: agricultural science, art education, home
economics, industrial arts, language arts, mathematics. In
the case of physical education, classes in the following
activities were taking place: campcraft, skiing, canoeing,
swimming, safety and survival, hiking, back packing, orienteering, open country games and individual sports. A health
education programme included the effects of pollution—air,
soil and water—on human health; the importance of outdoor education in maintaining fitness of mind and body;
health problems created by unrestricted population growth;
first aid; and accident prevention. The report showed that a
great amount was going on but coordination was needed if

the best use of facilities and a sharing of experiences was to be achieved.

In England, similar work is going on but perhaps we are in need of a similar study so that some sort of coordination of this good work can be achieved. J. M. Parker and K. I. Meldrum (1973) have begun this task in a recent book but it needs developing.

A large number of Education Authorities now boast at least one outdoor education centre and often a specialised centre for adventurous activities in mountains. There appears, however, to be a reaction against the large, expensive, well-staffed centre and many schools own centres often converted and equipped by their own efforts, and in this way have been able to establish a very worthwhile programme of outdoor education catering for their own particular needs.

One school in central London, without its own centre or easy access to an authority one, organises a flourishing Outdoor Pursuits Club with a very full diary of events as is shown by this extract from their diary for the Autumn term 1973.

September
Rock climbing at Harrison's Rocks, Sussex.
Duke of Edinburgh's Award Bronze expedition—Derbyshire.
October
Coastal camp at Durdle Door, Dorset.
Fishing excursion to Portsmouth.
November
Fishing excursion—Upper Thames.
Duke of Edinburgh's Award Silver and Gold level assessment.
Brecon Beacons, South Wales.
Orienteering course at a rural centre in Sussex.
Long distance walk—Pilgrims' Way (Hindhead to Canterbury).
December
Rock climbing at Harrison's Rocks, Sussex.
Orienteering course at a rural centre in Sussex.
Fishing excursion to Norfolk.

Similar programmes are planned for the other terms of the year and a more adventurous expedition to Iceland has been planned for the summer holiday. In this, and similar ways, schools, even in urban areas, are setting up their own outdoor education programmes using facilities near and far and so adding to the experiences of their students.

An integrated approach to curriculum development in a mixed comprehensive school

Although the physical education programme discussed earlier was for a mixed comprehensive school and dance was part of the programme, the boys' and girls' physical education departments each had their own separate programmes. Another mixed comprehensive school began its life with a similar programme but by a process of on-going curriculum development, moved fairly quickly towards becoming an integrated department. The starting point was the clear need to pool the skills and interests of both men and women staff, in order to extend the range of options available to older students; this was achieved in the second year of the school's life. In the next year the boys' department introduced dance for the first-year boys and this culminated in a joint dance production at one of the school functions. As this was judged to be a success, and as there had been an unnecessary duplication of effort by men and women staff teaching dance, gymnastics and swimming to single-sex classes, it was decided that the next first-year intake would be fully integrated.

Each double class was divided into three groups so that, with two physical education lessons per week the programme ran as shown in Table 6.1.

Each class then did dance, gymnastics and swimming for two lessons per week each term; and, because of the pooling of men and women staff, there were three members of staff for each double class and, consequently, fairly small groups were possible.

In the next school year, the fourth in the life of the school, the on-going curriculum development was carried a stage

TABLE 6.1 PHYSICAL EDUCATION PROGRAMME FOR A MIXED DOUBLE-CLASS DIVIDED INTO THREE GROUPS

	Dance	Gymnastics	Swimming
TERM 1	Group 1	Group 2	Group 3
TERM 2	Group 3	Group 1	Group 2
TERM 3	Group 2	Group 3	Group 1

further. The physical education department looked beyond its boundaries and, by combining with the drama, art and music departments, moved towards an integrated programme of creative arts for first-year pupils. Two groups of first-year pupils were allocated blocks of four lessons of dance, drama, art and music during one session of the school day. A team teaching situation was evolved in which topics were discussed by the teacher from the different departments who each presented it to the pupils from his own perspective for a period before passing them on to another teacher. The groups then came together to share their experiences.

The educational advantages of this integrated approach to the curriculum are not easy to evaluate. Groups are smaller and almost certainly have the opportunity to be involved in a greater width of movement and other creative experience than would otherwise have been possible. There are disadvantages, however, and not least is the demands made upon the staff involved; they need to be flexible and resourceful and, temporarily at least, be willing to replace their subject commitment with inter-disciplinary, team commitment. This is not easy, and it would be nice to report that this was achieved in the situation just described. However, as in all 'applied' curriculum development, certain realities of the school situation, not always perceived or taken into account by academic curriculum developers, take a hand and a promising development never reaches the stage where it can be properly evaluated.

In this case one happy and wholly positive, but interestingly enough, unperceived result, was the marriage of the man and woman physical educationists involved, an objective that could not possibly have been stated at the outset but which is easily evaluated at the end! However, they left the school soon afterwards and the experiment came to an end because their successors were not committed to it.

Departmental exchange

That curriculum development is inseparable from teacher development and that schools themselves, either independently or in cooperation with others, must create the conditions in which teachers can develop is so blindingly obvious that it is surprising that so much in-service training of teachers originates from outside schools and is therefore relatively ineffective. The following description of a piece of teacher development (at head of department level) suggests that similar, easily organised and inexpensive methods might yield greater returns than more complex and expensive methods.

Two heads of department, during informal discussion following an inter-school athletics match (not, it should be noted, at a conference on curriculum development, or even at a teachers' centre) decided that it might be useful if they changed schools for a short period so that they might compare how they had tackled common problems. They hoped that the experience would return them to their own teaching situations with new ideas and insights. In fact, they delegated the running of the two departments to their seconds in command and exchanged at a purely teaching level. In this way they hoped to gain deeper insights into the working of each department.

Both teachers worked in large comprehensive schools in urban situations with modest facilities on-site but very limited for team games. They had tackled this latter problem quite differently, one opting for a programme of single on-site physical education periods and afternoon game-sessions off-site on grass fields, and the other for a programme based on the maximum utilisation of on-site facilities using four single periods a week.

They defined the objectives of the exercise as:

(a) to examine the main difficulties of departmental organ-
    isation and administration;
(b) to discuss possible ways of improving their own
    individual situations.

After a week doing each other's jobs (almost certainly too
short a time) they had a long discussion and felt that they
had gained some useful experience in the following areas:

(a) Problems, which were clearly not evident to the
    teacher 'submerged' in his own department, had been
    brought to light. For example, it became clear to one
    head of department that he was providing options
    which were not numerically viable and consequently
    did not fully utilise highly-specialist teachers.
(b) Both heads of department had found alternative ways
    of tackling similar problems which could be tried out
    when they returned to their own schools. For example,
    the wet-weather programme of the school using off-
    site grass pitches might be modified in the light of the
    experience gained at a school using on-site facilities
    more systematically.
(c) On a personal level both heads of department found a
    new lease of life from the experience of working in
    environments with different programme facilities and,
    above all, different children.
(d) The second in command in each department was able
    to taste the responsibility of running a department.

Catering for children with special ability

The definition at the beginning of this chapter deliberately
included both local education authorities as well as the
individual school as agencies that might bring about changes
in pupils and the following description of a scheme to cater
for children with special ability demonstrates that the
resources of a single school are not adequate to cater for
children of exceptional ability in a wide range of activities.

The objects of this particular scheme are summed up in a

quotation from Schools Council Working Paper No. 37. It says:

> There can be no doubt that the future Olympic contestants should be 'spotted' in the middle years of schooling; the swimmers need to be identified near the beginning of the age range. Can the schools cope with the specialised training such children need if they are to achieve their potential? It may be that the education service should take a more positive part in such work and that there should be a series of optional (to the children) Saturday morning classes, or more properly training sessions, sponsored by the local authorities with specialist teachers undertaking these—for additional remuneration—as part of their ordinary work as teachers of physical education. There would seem to be no reason why each conurbation should not provide a whole series of Saturday morning classes for gifted and other children requiring additional facilities across the whole curriculum. The children's needs, the facilities, the accommodation, and the teacher's skills are all there; all that is needed is the financial resources and the organising.

It was decided, in this Local Education Authority, to operate the classes from 4.30 to 6.30 p.m. on two evenings a week and the classes were geographically situated to be accessible to as many children as possible. In the first instance Olympic Gymnastics classes were set up at four centres, fencing at two centres and diving and trampolining at one centre. Since then four judo classes have been started and it is proposed to set up other classes as a demand is perceived.

Selecting the children presented problems and certain criteria which included an age limit of thirteen and a fairly high level of initial ability were formulated. It was decided to leave the assessment of ability to physical education teachers in secondary schools and physical education advisers in primary schools and, although this created problems of standardisation, it is preferred to the use of such standardised tests as are available or might be devised.

Needless to say, the staff employed at these centres are highly qualified, are paid appropriately and are only expected to coach very small groups of children. They have been provided with the best facilities and equipment.

There have been problems. Some pupils have found the

cost of travelling to be excessive and the parents of others have been unhappy about their children being out fairly late on dark winter nights. The solution to both these problems is, possibly, centres catering for smaller geographical areas; but then the classes might not be of the very high standard envisaged and there will almost certainly be a shortage of highly qualified coaches.

Perhaps there ought to be two types of centre, one serving the locality and another to satisfy regional needs for intensive sessions at week-ends and perhaps travelling expenses should be paid. Such local and regional arrangements might even eventually be integrated into a national scheme and might go some way to answering those who claim that we don't cater properly for our talented children in this country. Equally, it would provide ammunition for those who oppose any form of elitism.

Physical education as a General Studies topic for the sixth form

Earlier I described some programmes stimulated by the raising of the school leaving age, and underlying most of the programmes developed at local authority level under the ROSLA banner is the assumption, now increasingly under attack, that the pupils for whom the work is designed will leave school at sixteen. Of course many of them will; but, as the immediate shock of the raising of the school leaving age recedes and short-term emergency programmes cease to be devised, most children might be allowed to follow a rationally worked out physical education programme which assumes that many of them will want to pursue (and will be competent to pursue) some aspect of the subject at a serious academic level in the sixth form. The programme which follows to some extent anticipates such a situation.

Within the context of an existing General Studies programme in a community college which catered for such wide-ranging courses as silversmithing, sociology, politics and computer studies, the physical education department decided (a) to institute a course using topics, falling under the general heading of physical education, which would extend the students' insight into the whole of society (its make-up, problems and values) and (b) to encourage independent inquiry and the drawing of accurate conclusions.

The course offered fell into three main areas, *human performance*, *sport and society*, and *first aid*, each area being allotted a two-lesson unit of eighty minutes. The human performance area consisted of laboratory visits, practical sessions, seminars and tutorials and was primarily concerned with the scientific examination and assessment of physical fitness, fatigue attention and arousal, motor skill and motivation.

So that the students would not get bogged down in pure theory the approach to these factors of human performance was based on the analysis of observable activities such as the performance of a footballer or athlete. Even so the teacher responsible for this area was pleasantly surprised at the ease with which students came to grips with such concepts as arousal theory, single channel theory and feedback principles.

The sport and society area of the course concentrated on an investigation of the interaction of sport and society in the modern world; discussions and seminars covered such topics as the effects of race, politics, nationalism and spectation on sport, the roles of amateur and professional sportsmen and sport as show business. Surveys of recreational activities and facilities were carried out and extended forwards into prediction about future requirements.

The first aid course was dropped after one year as it was felt that it could more appropriately be covered elsewhere in the lower-school physical education programme. The other two areas were, however, modified in the light of experience and pursued even more enthusiastically in the second year. The main conclusion that both teachers came to and which largely determined the modifications made, was the need to allow more time for the students themselves to investigate worthwhile problems in more depth; and the second year programme was, therefore, heavily orientated towards group and/or individual research. This approach presents few problems in the sociological area but the financial implications in the human performance area which needs fairly sophisticated equipment, are worrying. However, a laboratory using basic equipment is being built up and some students are engaged in developing a single-item test as an objective measure of soccer skill, while another is investigating the relationship between fitness, vital capacity and heart rates.

It is hoped as a result of two years' experience to develop CSE Mode III and CEE Mode III examinations in physical education and a CSE Mode III examination in physical recreation for less able children. This raises the whole question of examinations in physical education which deserves a chapter to itself but, in passing, it should be noted that CSE Mode III examinations in physical education and dance are now well established in this country and there appears to be less opposition in the profession to examinations than there was only a short time ago. However three interrelated questions still need answers before the fairly haphazard growth of examinations in physical education is given any further impetus:

(a) Is there sufficient agreement on the objectives and content of physical education to make a standardised public examination possible? If the answer to this question is 'Yes', then see (b).
(b) Is an examination in physical education desirable for the whole secondary school or only part of it? If the answer is 'part only' then see (c).
(c) Is the present or proposed examination system for school leavers at 16 capable of accommodating physical education or would an entirely different framework have to be devised.

As a postscript it should be mentioned that the experiment just described complements the normal physical education programme, sixth form options, outside clubs, etc., and will ultimately, one hopes, be an integral part of more rationally conceived programmes of physical education.

An Activities Field in a secondary school

This innovation has, quite deliberately, been left to the last because it demonstrates most vividly the kind of curriculum development that will occur in schools because of the sheer enthusiasm and ingenuity of individual teachers unconcerned with the jargon of 'pure' higher-education based 'curriculum mongers'. Such teachers are often blissfully unaware of the constraints sociologically orientated researchers assume hinder the implementation of innovations.

A young head of a physical education department was disappointed to learn from his headmaster that the new indoor facilities he had been promised were victims of yet another financial squeeze. Instead he could have further playing-fields. The school already had sufficient pitches for major games, so he decided to use part, at least, of the new field allocated to him to develop something completely new which would enlarge the range of activities he could offer to his pupils and also take some of the load off the over-burdened indoor facilities. So the Activities Field came into being.

The young teacher defined an Activities Field as 'an area specifically planned to include several outdoor activities that can be offered in a restricted space, to a class of average size and yet be supervised by a minimum of staff'. Armed with this definition he drew up a long list of activities he would like to include in such an area and then, mainly because of financial factors reduced it to a short list of four activities: athletics, golf, cyclo-cross and fitness.

The plan for the Activities Field was drawn up (Figure 6.2). The whole area of approximately 180 ft × 70 ft was divided into four main areas:

(a) *Jumping complex*, approximately 65 × 30 ft, including a large pit approachable from three sides and an all-weather take-off area allowing access to the pits for long and triple jump.
(b) *Training/assault course* (primarily for fitness training), including artificial ditches and ramps, to be built with the help of the army.

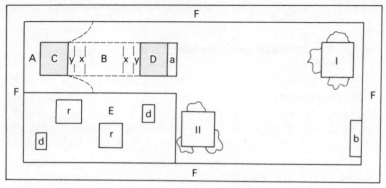

Figure 6.2   Activities field

A, B	Redgras areas for jumping complex	x	triple jump take-off
		y	long jump take-off boards
C, D	Sandpit landing areas	d	ditches
E	Training area/assault course	r	ramps
F	Cyclo-cross course	a, b	tee areas
I, II	Golf tees and bunkers		

(c) *Golf area* to include two teeing areas (probably artificial), to greens and three bunkers round each green.

(d) *Cyclo-cross area* to surround the field as an uneven, banked course 15 ft wide.

It is fair to add that this innovation is in its very early stages and the field is still in the course of construction. It does, however, as suggested earlier, demonstrate that much curriculum innovation arises out of the needs, opportunities and perceptions of teachers in their own teaching situations rather than from some theoretical model.

References

CHAPMAN, G. F. (1972) 'A new look at the physical education programme'. *ILEA Physical Education Journal*, Spring term.

MCNAB, T. (1970) *Modern School Athletics.* University of London Press: London.

PARKER, T. M. and MELDRUM, K. I. (1973) *Outdoor Education.* Dent: London.

Schools Council Working Paper 37 (1971). *Physical Education 8–13.* Evans/Methuen: London.

CHAPTER SEVEN

Effecting Change in the Physical Education Curriculum

Neville J. Whitehead

So that the mechanism of curriculum change in England may be understood, it is necessary to outline the present mode of control. The central government directs and controls education through its Department of Education and Science. The Department employs a body of people, Her Majesty's Inspectors who advise the Minister of State responsible for the Department of Education and Science. But with the exception of the case of religious education, the Department does not directly interfere with the arrangements made for the curriculum by schools or other educational institutions.

In the counties or metropolitan districts, local education authorities are elected and they are responsible for education in their areas. The LEAs appoint a chief education officer and a permanent staff to assist him. But these intervene only indirectly in curriculum matters. Therefore the power to decide the content of the curriculum in English schools lies theoretically in the hands of the schools' headteachers.

The headteachers have the freedom to determine the subjects taught, how much timetable time to allocate to various subjects, which books and equipment to buy, and which staff shall teach the various classes. Headteachers are advised by school governors (laymen appointed from within the locality), but the headteachers rely more on the advice of their staff. In fact, though it may appear that the headteacher has great power, the school teacher also has great freedom. For though he must teach that to which he is assigned on the timetable, the content of the lessons are of his own choice.

It could be said that the physical education teacher has even greater freedom than teachers of other subjects. For the latter may be directed towards teaching particular subject content systematically in preparing children for examinations, and the effectiveness of his teaching may well be measured by the success of the pupils in the examinations. But the physical education teacher rarely has to make explicit to his employers, colleagues, or the children's parents, what he is teaching and why he is teaching it. Furthermore, except in the case of those who organise inter-school games fixtures, the success of the physical education teacher's work is not easily measurable by the outsider.

Recent researches in England have highlighted the need for curriculum improvement in physical education in junior, middle and secondary schools (Whitehead, 1969; Dolman, 1970; Coutts, 1970; Rowe, 1970); this chapter discusses how the changes might be effected and the difficulties likely to be encountered.

The curriculum process

In recent years, innovation in physical education in England appears to have been more the result of efforts by enthusiastic individuals than considered planning and research. Changes have mainly been in the nature of the content of physical education lessons, and they have not always been accompanied by evidence to justify the changes made. Davies (1966) has suggested that the reason for this is that colleges of education courses for student physical education teachers do not 'challenge their minds', and he is of the opinion that physical educationists should give deeper thought to the reasons why they teach the various aspects of their subject. He writes:

> Am I right in suspecting that a clear understanding of the aims of physical education may be untypical of many college lecturers, that to many, the aims are self-evident and arise naturally from the situation

in which they find themselves, and that the whole nature of their own training works against a willingness to make these aims explicit and fundamental to their task?

Hoyle (1969) has stated that a proposal for changing curricula implies that a case has been made for a need for change, whereas Taba (1962) has stated that one of the problems related to changing curricula is that the process necessitates a change in people and institutions. It would appear, therefore, that when planning to effect change in a physical education curriculum, the process needs to:

(a) include an evaluation of the present curriculum;
(b) present a case based on sound principles for the improvement of the curriculum;
(c) estimate the difficulties that might be encountered in the changes, including the people affected; and
(d) ensure that the proposals include the requirement of the need for continual evaluation of the curriculum.

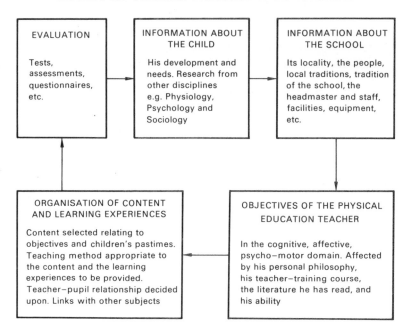

Figure 7.1   The physical education curriculum process

A diagrammatic representation of this process appears in Figure 7·1.

Curriculum strategies

The curriculum process involved in implementing change can be put into effect by the use of a number of different strategies which entail the involvement of a number of different participants at different times. The main strategies that would appear to be employable to effect changes in physical education curricula are:

(1) by evaluation and implementation of research findings;
(2) by Central Government direction;
(3) by changes in physical education teacher-training;
(4) by in-service education;
(5) by action taken within individual schools.

It has been pointed out that the strategies employed will differ from school to school, and even within any one school at different times (Doll, 1972). In a school where a recently qualified teacher has arrived, the changes in the curriculum may be the result of the new knowledge he has acquired during his teacher-training course and the closer cooperation he enjoys with the headmaster and staff compared with his predecessor. In another school, the change might result from the attendance of the physical education teacher on an in-service course which was recommended or organised by the local education authority's physical education inspectors.

The values and limitations of all of these strategies need to be studied by physical educationists, and in particular it should be understood that curriculum *change* is not necessarily curriculum *improvement*, neither is curriculum change or improvement always a *planned* venture. The various strategies are discussed in following pages in relation to the probability of their being used in England and the relative merits of each.

(1) Evaluation and implementation of research findings

Physical education teachers need to be continually reappraising the value of their own teaching and the content of their lessons, as well as revising their programmes in order to present more appropriate experiences for children in a changing society. It is relatively simple to administer tests to discover for instance if a child's 'fitness' is improving, or his 'strength' or his 'endurance' are increasing. It is also easy to discover objectively whether children are improving in their ability, say, in gymnastics and swimming. But it is also important for the teacher to find out what value particular experiences have for children, what their attitudes are towards the experiences and how they are affected by them. Though such information can be elicited by observation by the experienced teacher, and records made of his observations, when more accurate methods of collecting such data become available they should be used, e.g. personality inventories, attitude tests, questionnaires, etc. This important aspect of accurate evaluation ensures not only that the success of the teachers' objectives is being judged, but that records are being kept of how the children are growing and developing throughout their school careers.

Research evidence is available to show that physical activity makes an important contribution in human development. Jean Piaget (1950 and 1951) has stressed the importance of physical activity in the development of the intellect. Other psychologists have emphasised that in the learning process, a child's progress needs to be explained in terms of external influences as well as the internal processes (Bruner, 1966; White, 1959). Recent emphases appear to have been on the fact that with children, things are lived rather than thought and that there is a reliance early in a child's life on movement experience (Bruner, 1967; Vygotsky, 1962).

The implications of the work of Piaget and many other investigations have been summarised (Burgess, 1965) and the importance of motor experience, playing games with children, and providing stimulating and diversified learning experiences, have all been shown to be important platforms for learning. A summary of the research findings related to physical activity has shown also how physical activity may specifically assist in the changing of attitudes, improving social efficiency, improving sensory perception and assisting in mental health as well as in the acquisition of skill (Scott, 1960). In addition, researches have reported the sociological values of sport (Biddulph, 1954; Yukie, 1955; Bentsen *et al.*, 1955). Other evidence has been produced to show that present-day physical education specialists may make contributions in the field of special education, additional to their roles as sports coaches (Oliver, 1958 and 1960). Thus a wealth of literature may be found pointing to the mental and social as well as the physiological benefits to be derived from physical activity. But authors of physical education literature in England do not always quote such researches. It often appears to be the case that authors simply state their own views based on their own experiences.

Examples of this have been seen in recent years in the introduction of 'educational gymnastics' or 'basic movement' into English schools. Numerous books have been written on the subject with claims for the value of work including:

> The Basic Movement approach is aimed at training the child's kinaesthetic sense. (Randall, 1961)
> The work is based on natural activities. Mobility is maintained, coordination is developed and the correct application of strength is encouraged. (Cameron and Pleasance, 1963)

However, the work is not without its critics:

> I personally never see this work (educational gymnastics) with older children or students without becoming bored and feeling how much more the able ones could be challenged. (Munrow, 1963)

Furthermore, researches have shown that the men and women teachers in the schools tend to concur with Munrow, and limit the teaching of educational gymnastics to the younger children in schools despite the claims for the value of the work (Whitehead, 1969; Rowe, 1970).

On the subject of 'modern educational dance' too there

seem to have been possible overstatements of its value to children, including:

> Dance has been found to be a means of expression which all can explore immediately and naturally and more easily than written English, Drama, and the other arts . . . (Russell, 1958).

However, teachers in schools tend not to include a great deal of modern educational dance in their programmes (Whitehead, 1969; Rowe, 1970), but the emphases within modern physical education result in some expression of concern:

> Men have retained the developmental objectives . . . Women . . . regard physical or developmental effects as a by-product. (Munrow, 1963)

Mason (1970) appears to have proffered sound advice to teachers when he reminded them that it is incorrect to believe that *activities* have a particular effect upon children: it is the *teacher* who influences and who ensures that particular effects are forthcoming from participation in physical activity.

It could be said, therefore, that research findings from other disciplines are available which illustrate the value of physical activity at different stages of a child's life. What appears to be needed is a rational application of these findings in physical education, and a more cautionary view of other proposals for curriculum change which tend to be based more on personal belief than on research or experimentation.

(2) *Central government direction*

Prior to World War II, the government's Board of Education published *Syllabuses of Physical Training (1904, 1905, 1909, 1919 and 1933)*. They stated the aims and objectives of the subject at the time, in the view of the Board's physical education inspectors, and the syllabuses included tables of lessons and games activities which might have enabled the teacher to achieve those objectives.

After the war, however, the Ministry of Education's publication in 1952 of *Moving and Growing* and *Planning the Programme* (to replace the 1933 Syllabus of Physical Training) marked one of the landmarks in the history of English physical education. The Ministry no longer stated the objectives of the subject and the publications include no tables of lessons for teachers to follow. Furthermore, it not only entailed less direction of the teachers' efforts in physical education, but it also emphasised the importance of a new informal approach in the teaching of the subject:

> These then are the various opportunities we might expect to find.
> (Ministry of Education, 1952)

The Department of Education and Science (1972) publication *Movement* superseded these two publications, but emphasised similar purposes of physical education:

> It is the role of physical education to offer ... varied movement experiences ...

There were no tables of lessons contained in this latest publication. Thus the government nowadays tends not to direct what is to be taught, but by inference can make known what the Inspectorate believe to be of value. For instance, the literature published by the Department of Education and Science has made it clear what the Department considers should be happening in the new 'middle schools':

> There is a broad general agreement that class teachers throughout the school should take their own classes for a large proportion of the time. (DES, 1970a)

and:

> Experience in the few middle schools now open suggest that it may prove feasible to have mixed groups for all physical education save for some games and athletics. (DES, 1970b)

That is, the Department does not necessarily expect a physical education specialist to be teaching the subject throughout the middle schools, and boys and girls can be mixed for most physical education lessons.

On the subject of the content of physical education lessons, the Schools Council publications have made more precise recommendations.

1. Educational gymnastics and educational dance should be the basis of indoor work for boys and girls.
2. The development of games-skills leading to small-side team games, thence to minor games, thence perhaps to modified versions of major games should be the basis of outdoor work. (DES, 1971)

In addition to the publications, the Department can make its views known by organising in-service courses and during its Inspectors' visits to educational institutions. However, in recent years, the policy of the Department has been to permit more autonomy for the teachers and the schools, and for there to be less direction by the central government on the subject of curriculum content.

(3) Physical education teacher-training

Both Whitehead (1969) and Follows (1972) have illustrated how men and women physical education teachers in the early years of their teaching tend to rely on teaching those activities which they themselves experienced during their college careers. This fact emphasises the importance of colleges selecting appropriate activities based on careful consideration of schoolchildren's needs. But some educationists doubt whether physical education students in colleges of education are in fact being provided with appropriate studies. Davies (1966) puts it like this:

> What are difficult to assess are the attitudes of lecturers in physical education departments, the emphases which are given to different parts of the syllabuses, the degree to which these men and women are genuinely interested in physical education rather than in being experts in the physical. Since they too are drawn from the ranks of those who have achieved high personal standards in physical activities, it is possible that printed syllabuses are weighted towards the practical and against the philosophical.

Whitehead (1969) and Follows (1972) showed that men's and women's physical education courses differed radically among the colleges. In one college the emphasis might be on outdoor activities, in another on dance and in another on physiological aspects. In these and other researches, teachers have been quoted as being critical of their college courses as a preparation for their physical education curriculum planning and organisation in schools.

But in addition to the twenty-five 'specialist physical education colleges' there are a further seventy colleges which offer physical education as a 'main' subject. Students in colleges can also study physical education as a 'second' or 'subsidiary' subject. Additionally, students can attend courses to become qualified physical education teachers at two universities, and an increasing number of polytechnics are beginning to offer physical education courses at first-degree level and qualified teacher status.

Thus it would appear to be unrealistic to expect national agreement on curriculum content from so many diverse institutions. Furthermore, the current reorganisation of higher education in England seems to be resulting in the structure of the present three-year teacher-training courses, in which emphasis on the pedagogical aspects of physical education normally continues throughout the three years, becoming a two-year study of the 'academic' aspects of physical education followed by a one-year professional training course. It is difficult to estimate how the reorganisation will affect the nature of the teachers who go into the schools in future years, but it could be conjectured that in the planning of new courses, there is not necessarily likely to be any greater similarity in the new courses than there has been in the past.

Nevertheless, teacher-training courses can result in the teachers effecting change in schools' physical education curricula; for instance, when a teacher arrives at a new appointment and was trained at a different college from that of his predecessor. Curriculum change can also result when schools' large physical education departments consist of teachers trained at a number of different institutions. But planning to ensure change in physical education curricula in schools will normally be a decision of individual colleges and not necessarily an agreed policy among all the colleges at any one time.

(4) In-service education

In-service courses in England for physical education teachers are of three main types:

(a) those provided by the Department of Education and Science;
(b) those provided by local education authority inspectors; and
(c) those provided by other bodies, such as university departments, governing bodies of various sports and individual colleges.

The role of the Department of Education and Science has been described in this way:

> The Minister is required to cause inspections to be made of every educational establishment at appropriate intervals, or to satisfy himself that there are other suitable arrangements. (DES, 1968)

On the subject of provision of courses, it would appear that the Department do organise a number of short courses, but appear to be satisfied 'that there are other suitable arrangements', because the majority of courses are organised by local education authorities and other bodies, with the Department publishing a booklet on 'approved' courses, i.e. those which have the support of the Department. These range from one-year courses of 'advanced diploma' level at universities to shorter-term courses. The former include some physical education courses, but are predominantly courses in 'Education', while the remainder are mainly short courses offered during vacations.

Local authorities' physical education inspectors also offer evening, weekend and vacation courses for the teachers within their areas. The subject of the courses depends upon the needs in the various schools in the authority; they are staffed by the inspectors, sometimes with help from teachers or 'experts' in particular fields, attendance is not compulsory, and teachers get no recognition for attending them in the form of certificates, salary increases or promotion (it is recognised, however, that regular course-attenders may have the advantage when applying for vacancies if they make it known to appointing committees the fact that they have attended numerous courses). As a means of curriculum improvement, it could be said that the brevity of the courses ensures that only elementary details of new activities are expatiated, and teachers would only be able to sustain long periods of new work in their schools' programmes if regular guidance and visits were forthcoming from the local authority inspectors. Normally, such follow-up is not always possible.

The largest group of courses for physical education teachers are those organised by governing bodies in preparation for specific coaching awards, e.g. Amateur Athletic Association, Football Association, Amateur Swimming Association, Lawn Tennis Association and MCC cricket courses, etc. The emphases of these courses are predominantly on the improvement of skill of the individual on the games field, track or in the swimming pool, and they include little or no reference to teaching the activities to schoolchildren. Even the large, popular one-week and two-weeks vacation courses consist mainly of governing-body award courses, and not all local authorities will pay the expenses of teachers to attend the courses. Therefore course attending often becomes the habit of keen individuals rather than those in need of acquiring new knowledge, and governing-body courses may not necessarily be considered appropriate or effective vehicles for curriculum improvement.

(5) Individual schools

Beauchamp (1968) has described the value of the individual school as the centre for curriculum planning thus:

> The 'beauty' of the situation is that the individuals who develop the curriculum strategies are the same ones who develop and carry out the instructional strategies.

But it could be said that the situation would not be so 'beautiful' if the programmes of physical education presented to the children were based on the teachers' interests and account were not taken of the nature of the children, their needs, and the external influences that affected them. In other words, the 'beauty' would be more likely if teachers adopted a curriculum planning process similar to that illustrated in Figure 7.1 (p. 167).

At the present time, it would appear that the most effective strategy to improve physical education curricula in England would be the individual school-based strategy, to be supported eventually by locally-based curriculum study groups. In the meantime, the Department of Education and Science or the Schools Council could assist by publishing literature illustrating the process by which individual schools could begin to improve their physical education programmes.

Improving programmes

The physical education teacher's philosophy

Williams (1968) has indicated what he considers should be one of the foremost thoughts in any physical educationist's mind:

> The essential problem before the student or teachers of physical education is to arrive at a point of view that he can live with, acquire an attitude that he can support and, if necessary defend.

But Percival (1967) has intimated that he believes English physical education teachers to be more interested in teaching good performers than considering the purpose of what they should be doing. It is imperative for curriculum improvement that teachers should give a great deal of consideration to the relevance of the content of their physical education programmes and not select haphazardly the activities to present to their pupils.

Satisfying the needs of the pupils

A good physical education teacher will not only understand the needs of children at different stages of physiological and psychological growth, he will also take into account the ongoing research into child development, he will study the people in the community in which the school is situated, and he will ascertain the nature of employment and leisure activities of the local inhabitants.

He will determine how, via the medium of physical education, he can help to satisfy the unique needs of each of the children in the school, whether they be clever or clumsy, reluctant or willing. His physical education programmes will be designed not only to cater for the children when they are pupils, but also aim to inculcate a will to participate in physical activity after their school life.

Establishing objectives

Every physical education teacher should be able to make explicit that which he is attempting to achieve when teaching his subject. The objectives will differ from school to school, dependent upon the teacher's philosophy, the children's needs, and the locality of the school. But the only method by which a physical education programme's success can be measured is by relating its outcome to its intended effect.

Having established objectives, the physical education teacher then has to decide upon which of them to place the stronger emphases. For his time-allocation to different activities will reflect the more important objectives that he is attempting to achieve. Especially in the early years of his teaching career, he may well rely on other sources in preference to his own judgment when deciding what his objectives should be.

External assistance

Not only will the physical education teachers study literature on school programmes and the opinion of 'authorities'

on physical education curricula, they should be prepare
exchange visits with teachers from other schools to ascer
how they have solved their problems.

In well-organised areas, such exchange of information
takes place under the chairmanship of local inspectors. But
the fact that such meetings are not arranged, ought not to
prevent individual teachers from ensuring that they share
their expertise and glean useful information from other
teachers in local schools, or even faraway schools with
similar circumstances to their own.

Internal decisions

Should a physical education teacher be one of a large department of specialists, an obvious source of aid to him in
curriculum planning would be departmental meetings. Short
meetings could provide a wealth of expertise and opinion.
Such meetings should be regularly held, preferably at times
when staff are not preoccupied with other matters, and
should aim not at evaluating or planning the whole school
programme, but at permitting discussion on one small part
of it. They could also be the means for sub-groups to be
formed to look into one particular problem, or minor
research projects could result that would be of value to the
school and other physical education teachers.

These meetings should not be combined with other
departmental business; in fact, teachers of other subjects
who assist in the work of the department could be invited
and might well make valuable contributions.

Planning a programme

When commencing the planning of his physical education
programme, the teacher has no simple task. In addition to
teaching skills and disseminating knowledge, the teacher's
responsibility includes the attempt to inculcate certain attitudes in the schoolchildren and to ensure that particular
experiences and relationships are provided for them. The
purposes of these experiences are numerous and vary

among schools, but they include ensuring that the normally dependent child is confronted with situations in which he needs to be independent; the normally aggressive child be required to control his aggression; the intolerant child be required to practise tolerance; the domineering child be required to be more submissive; the fearful child be assisted in being more courageous; the less cautious child be required to be more restrained and the hard child to be more sympathetic.

These experiences might normally be expected to be provided incidentally by the good teacher, but all physical education teachers ought to be impressed to plan to include them in their programmes and not simply to select activities regardless of the situations which might arise in them.

The selection and organising of the content of the physical education programmes will be related to the teacher's expectation of the outcome of the programme in terms of satisfying children's needs and having a particular effect upon them when taught by particular teachers. It should not be based on the belief that some activities are necessarily more 'educational' than others. Neither should the activities selected be organised in the traditional single- or double-period system without a reconsideration of the value of this method of allocation of time. Serious thought should be given to what ought to be the core of the programme; what 'options' should be offered and at what age; the implications of the extra-curricular activity including games teams and week-end camps; the possibility of links with other subject areas, and relationships with other schools.

The organisational pattern of the programme should include consideration of the nature of the teaching groups; the arrangements for boys' and girls' classes; whether or not 'mixed ability' groups are to be employed, and staff deployment. In situations where non-specialist staff are to assist, the decision has to be taken about where their particular expertise would be most beneficial to the children. Additionally, it would have to be decided whether the physical education staff will be required to specialise in one or two areas of work, or whether the best effect would result from their being employed as 'jacks-of-all-trades'.

Finally, consideration will be given to the effects of constraints on the curriculum of finance, accommodation and equipment, and plans will be prepared for amending the programme should the need arise.

Revisions

Physical education, like other subjects, is continually in the process of change, and teachers should therefore consider their programmes as experiments to be evaluated throughout the academic year, and revised frequently to take into account new knowledge and changing circumstances, with an ever-present striving for improvement.

Conclusion

In planning curricula, teachers are confronted by a number of difficulties that limit their choice; some of the problems are general to all subjects, whereas some are peculiar to physical education.

In physical education, one restraint upon curriculum improvement, it has been suggested, is the nature of the physical education teacher (Whitehead, 1973). In fact, both Ward (1967) and Whitehead (1973) have shown that the selection procedures for women's and men's places on physical education courses in England are based on similar criteria, viz. oral interview and practical performance tests, and these have been demonstrated as lacking validity and being unreliable predictors of students' future success in their college courses. In physical stature, physical educationists have been shown to tend to mesomorphy (Hendry, 1970), while they tend to score high on personality factors related to extraversion, stability and toughmindedness (Jones, 1970; Kane, 1968). But this assertive, rapid-action physical education teacher is not necessarily the precision worker who in modern times is likely to contemplate the point of view of others who may be in disagreement with him, and who are proposing change.

Furthermore, the college courses that the physical education teacher attends have been criticised for not 'challenging students' minds' (Davies, 1966); therefore these facts should be borne in mind by those who view curriculum change in physical education in England as a slow process.

Though headteachers often rely on physical education teachers' judgment on the choice of curriculum content, it should be remembered that the teachers are appointed usually by the headteachers; thus it could be said that those of similar views to the headteacher are likely to be appointed to schools' posts. Other headteachers remind the physical educationist of the school tradition, and insist for instance on rugby football to be played and not soccer (or vice versa). Similarly, headmasters' attitudes towards competition can affect physical education teachers' programme planning, so that the emphasis could occasionally be placed on good games teams and on winning cups and league competitions—not on catering for the needs of all boys. Headteachers can therefore be a help in supporting a good physical education teacher and supplying finance and equipment to ensure the success of his department, or they can be a hindrance.

The nature of the physical education teacher's role as educationist and coach results occasionally in conflict for him, as does the employment of the assistance of other staff to help him in both roles. A wide range of activities offered in a school depends on assistance for the physical education teacher from his colleagues; but such assistance needs to be carefully placed and closely controlled so that the assistants know to what end the particular parts of the programme are directed. Otherwise such assistance can become an opposing force to the department's objectives.

Another limitation on the teacher of physical education is the locality of the school. The obvious problems are for those schools in the middle of large cities where no facilities are available for outdoor pursuits. Additionally, there are schools in remote areas to which boys travel many miles each day and have to leave immediately after school in the evening, thus affecting the organisation of after-school activities.

An obvious further restraint on a physical education teacher's planning of an improved curriculum is the range of facilities and equipment available to him. If, for instance, the gymnasium is used as an assembly hall and dining hall, then the nature of the activities taught in it will probably exclude pupils' rolling around the floor at particular times of the day. Also affecting programme content will be whether expensive facilities have been bought by previous teachers at the school. If a swimming-pool is available, the headmaster will expect it to be used, or if weight-training equipment is available, it will be expected to be used, despite a new teacher's inability or lack of desire to incorporate such activities in his programme.

The role of the physical education inspector appointed by the local education authority is that of an adviser to head-teachers and physical education teachers. There are some authorities, however, in which the inspector bans particular activities and other activities which may only be taught if the teachers acquire governing body qualifications in addition to their teaching certificate. For example, some schools are unable to plan mountain activities unless the physical education teacher has a 'mountain leadership certificate', and other schools are forbidden to teach trampoline activities unless the physical education teacher has a trampoline federation certificate (often obtainable only after the teacher has left college and after attending a trampoline course). The physical education inspector's philosophy, interests, views on dangerous activities and control of finance may therefore have an effect upon the physical education curriculum of some schools.

The nature of a school's physical education programme and the range of activities offered will often depend upon the finance made available to the school by the local authority, and the proportion of that money passed to the physical education department by the headmaster. This is always tied to taxes and rates, in that the education that children get is

184 Curriculum Development in Physical Education

that which their parents are prepared to pay for. If the parents object to the raising of taxes, or rates, then the education budget is usually one that is cut. Finance also forces choice. If money is available, there could be a possible choice between a swimming pool or a sports hall. If a swimming-pool is built, then a wider range of aquatic sports would be possible, but less indoor games training.

Finally, the challenge that remains for physical educationists in England is to produce a better curriculum based on sound educational principles. The emphasis in the past on improving teaching methods seems to have been based on the assumption that physical education teachers knew why they were teaching that which they were teaching, but present-day improved research techniques are showing that this was not always so, and points to the fact that physical educationists must be continuously reviewing their beliefs and revising their programmes.

References

AHRENS, M. (1956) 'Parents and staff co-operate in system-wide improvement'. *Educational Leadership*, **II**, 450–51.

BEAUCHAMP, G. A. (1968) *Curriculum Theory*. The Kagg Press: Wilmette, Illinois, p. 124.

BENTSEN, T. B. and SUMMERSKILL, J. (1955) 'Relation of personal success in intercollegiate athletics to certain aspects of personal adjustment'. *Research Quarterly*, **26**, 8.

BIDDULPH, L. G. (1954) 'Athletic achievement versus the personal and social adjustment of high school boys'. *Research Quarterly*, **25**, 1.

BOARD OF EDUCATION (1902) *Model Course of Physical Training*. HMSO: London.

BOARD OF EDUCATION (1904) *Syllabus of Physical Exercises for Use in Elementary Schools*. HMSO: London.

BOARD OF EDUCATION (1909) *Syllabus of Physical Exercises for Schools*. HMSO: London.

BOARD OF EDUCATION (1919) *Syllabus of Physical Training for Schools*. HMSO: London.

BOARD OF EDUCATION (1933) *Syllabus of Physical Training for Schools*. HMSO: London.

BRUNER, J. S. (1966) *Toward a Theory of Instruction*. Harvard University Press: Cambridge, Massachusetts.

BRUNER, J. S. *et al.* (1967) *Studies in Cognitive Growth*. Wiley: New York.

BURGESS, F. (1965) *Values in Early Childhood Education*. National Education Association: Washington, DC.

CAMERON, W. M. and PLEASANCE, P. (1963) *Education in Movement*. Blackwell: Oxford, p. 4.

COUTTS, A. (1970) 'The new middle schools'. Unpublished diploma dissertation, University of Leeds.

DAVIES, H. (1966) 'The training of teachers of physical education'. BAOLPE *Bulletin*, **67**, 9–25.

DEPARTMENT OF EDUCATION AND SCIENCE (1968) *Report from the select Committee on Education and Science*. Part I. HMSO: London, p. iv.

DEPARTMENT OF EDUCATION AND SCIENCE (1970a) *Launching Middle Schools*. HMSO, p. 12.

DEPARTMENT OF EDUCATION AND SCIENCE (1970b) *Towards the Middle School*. HMSO, p. 28.

DEPARTMENT OF EDUCATION AND SCIENCE (1971) *Physical Education 8–13*, Schools Council Working Paper 37. HMSO: London, p. 35.

DEPARTMENT OF EDUCATION AND SCIENCE (1972) *Movement—Physical Education in the Primary Years*. HMSO: London, p. 8.

DOLL, R. C. (1972) *Curriculum Improvement: Decision-making and Process*. Allyn and Bacon: Boston, Massachusetts.

DOLMAN, D. (1970) 'Comparative aspects of primary schools' physical education'. Unpublished diploma dissertation, University of Leeds.

FOLLOWS, M. (1972) 'Physical education in middle years'. Unpublished diploma dissertation, University of Leeds.

HENDRY, L. B. (1970) 'A comparative analysis of student characteristics'. M.Ed thesis, University of Leicester.

HOYLE, E. (1969) 'How does the curriculum change?' *Journal of Curriculum Studies*, **1**, 239.

JONES, M. (1970) 'Perception, personality and movement'. M.Ed thesis, University of Leicester.

KANE, J. E. (1968) 'Personality in relation to physical ability and physique'. Ph.D. thesis, University of London.

MASON, M. (1970) 'Towards a theory of group action'. *Research Papers in Physical Education*, **9**, 8.

MINISTRY OF EDUCATION (1952) *Moving and Growing*. HMSO: London, p. 52.

MINISTRY OF EDUCATION (1953) *Planning the Programme*. HMSO: London.

MUNROW, A. D. (1963) *Pure and Applied Gymnastics*. Arnold: London, p. 277.

OLIVER, J. N. (1958) 'Effect of physical conditioning exercises and activities on the mental characteristics of educationally sub-normal boys'. *British Journal of Educational Psychology*, **28**, 155–65.

OLIVER, J. N. (1960) 'Effect of physical conditioning exercises on the sociometric status of educationally sub-normal boys'. *Physical Education*, **52**, 38–46.

PIAGET, J. (1950) *The Psychology of Intelligence*. Routledge and Kegan Paul: London.

PIAGET, J. (1951) *Play, Dreams and Imitation in Childhood*. Heinemann: London.

RANDALL, M. (1961) *Basic Movement*. Bell: London, p. 46.

ROWE, M. (1970) 'An examination of the physical education for boys and girls in secondary schools'. Unpublished diploma dissertation, University of Leeds.

RUSSELL, J. (1958) *Modern Dance in Education*. Macdonald and Evans: London, p. 80.

SCOTT, M. G. (1960) 'The contribution of physical activity to psychological development'. *Research Quarterly*, **31**, 2.

TABA, H. (1962) *Curriculum Development, Theory and Practice*. Harcourt, Brace and World; New York, p. 415.

VYGOTSKY, L. S. (1962) *Thought and Language*. MIT Press: Cambridge, Massachusetts.

WARD, B. P. (1967) 'The selection of applicants for courses in physical education'. *Research Papers in Physical Education*, **4**, 13.

WHITE, R. W. (1959) 'Motivation reconsidered: the concept of competence'. *Psychological Review*, **66**, 297–333.

WHITEHEAD, N. J. (1969) An examination of schools' and colleges' physical education syllabuses. Unpublished M.Ed thesis, University of Leicester.

WHITEHEAD, N. J. (1973) 'An examination of the selection procedures, final assessments and teaching careers of students in colleges of education'. Unpublished Ph.D thesis, University of Aston, Birmingham.

WILLIAMS, J. F. (1968) *The Principles of Physical Education*. Saunders: Philadelphia, p. 324.

YUKIE, E. C. (1955) 'Group movement and growth in a physical education class'. *Research Quarterly*, **26**, 222.

Index

Italic numerals refer to figures